THE TRUE CHURCH

The Multi-Dimensional Manifestation of the Real Church

ISAAK K. ARIKAWE

The True Church
Copyright © 2015 by Isaak K. Arikawe All rights reserved.

No part of this publication may be reproduced, stored in a retrieval system or transmitted in any way by any means, electronic, mechanical, photocopy, recording or otherwise, without the prior permission of the author except as provided by USA copyright law.

All characters appearing in this work are fictitious. Any resemblance to real persons, living or dead, is purely coincidental.

The opinions expressed by the author are not necessarily those of Revival Waves of Glory Books & Publishing.

Published by Revival Waves of Glory Books & Publishing
PO Box 596| Litchfield, Illinois 62056 USA
www.revivalwavesofgloryministries.com

Revival Waves of Glory Books & Publishing is committed to excellence in the publishing industry.

Book design copyright © 2015 by Revival Waves of Glory Books & Publishing. All rights reserved.

Paperback: 978-1-60796-598-5
Hardcover: 978-1-60796-599-2

Published in the United States of America

Table of Contents

Dedication 6
Endorsements 7
Appreciation 14
Author's Note 15
Introduction 16
Chapter One **The Birth of The Promised Church** 18
    THE CHURCH OF JESUS CHRIST 20
Chapter Two **The Church: A Spiritual Entity** 23
    THE MAJOR WORK OF HOLY SPIRIT WITHIN THE CHURCH 27
    THE PHILOSOPHY BEHIND JESUS' CHURCH 29
Chapter Three **The Church: The Body of Christ** 33
    A COMPLETE BEING 35
    ONE BODY, MANY PARTS 35
    DISCONNECTION EQUALS DEATH 39
    COVENANT RELATIONSHIP AND COMMUNITY LIVING WITHIN THE BODY 41
    JESUS, THE HEAD OF THE BODY 44
Chapter Four **The Church: The Bride of Christ** 46
    THE BRIDE'S (THE CHURCH) POSITION IN JESUS' LIFE 47
    THE NECESSARY CONDITIONS FOR THE MARRIAGE 49
    THE AFFECTION BETWEEN JESUS AND HIS BRIDE (THE CHURCH) 51
    ONE-SIDED AFFECTION 52
    DECEPTIVE HEART OF THE BRIDE 54

CHURCH: THE PROMISCUOUS LOVER 55

STANDARD FOR THE TRUE BRIDE 58

PRINCIPLES TO BE NOTED IN THESE SCRIPTURES 59

Chapter Five **The Church: The Temple of God** 63

GOD'S CONCEPT ABOUT TEMPLE 64

TEMPLE IN DISPENSATION 66

THE TEMPLE AND THE OLD COVENANT 67

THE DEFICIENCY OF OLD COVENANT TEMPLE 68

THE PATTERN OF THE NEW DISPENSATION TEMPLE 71

THE PRINCIPLES BEHIND THE NEW TEMPLE BUILDING 72

THE OFFICE OF THE PRIEST IN THE TEMPLE 75

Chapter Six **The Church: A House of Prayer** 81

PRAYER 83

PRAYER AS A MEDIUM OF COMMUNICATION 83

PRAYER AS A TOOL FOR DIVINE INTERVENTION 84

PRAYER IS THE KEY TO REVIVAL AND REFORMATION 85

PRAYER: THE KEY THAT UNLOCKS REVELATION. 87

PRAYER ALIGNS MEN'S HEARTS TO THE WILL OF GOD. 88

PRAYER, THE PLATFORM FOR INTERCESSION 90

PRAYER BRINGS PROPHETIC DIRECTION. 91

PRAYER PRECEDES POWER 92

PRAYER IS THE STAMP OF THE CHURCH 93

JESUS' PATTERN OF PRAYER 95

WHEN THE CHURCH PRAYS 99

PREPARE FOR WAR 101

DECLARING WAR 102

Chapter Seven **The Church: In The World** 105

    THE CHURCH AND THE DYING WORLD... 107

    THE CHURCH AS A ROLE MODEL 111

Chapter Eight **Beware of The Synagogue of Satan** 113

    THE ATTRIBUTES OF THE SYNAGOGUE OF SATAN 118

Chapter Nine **The Present-day Church** 123

    THE GREAT HAPPENINGS.. 124

About the Book... 127

About the Author.. 128

Other books by the Author... 129

Kingdom School of Ministry.. 134

Dedication

It will be nothing but a fraud to dedicate this work to any man. Therefore, this book is dedicated to the One who alone is the source of life and revelation- the Holy Spirit- for revealing the mind of God for this hour.

To the people of God all over the world, who are addicted to the truth, not just by preaching it, but by living according to its principles and preparing the way for the coming of the Lord. I pray you will not build in vain.

Endorsements

A famous musician stopped singing in his early 50s and was asked why he did so, he said, " I have nothing more to talk or sing about"Isaac Arikawe still have more to say on the issues concerning the church. His choice of words and in-depth teaching in this book are vital to walking with God and Repairing the Broken walls in the body of Christ today. A job well done. Stay on top!

Olu Fred Kehinde
Presiding Bishop,
Power House Chapel International,
Cologne, Germany

The books; THE DEAD-LIVING CHURCH & the volume 2 THE TRUE CHURCH are revelatory materials for the church workers and ministers that are ready to understand the full concept of the Real Church; the Ecclesia which Jesus said he would build. This book also exposes the strategies of the devil within the Church. This book is a must read for anyone that desires to please God in their living.

Dr. D. K. Olukoya,
General Overseer,
Mountain of Fire & Miracles Ministries

Jesus is coming for a glorious Church adorned with beauty and majesty to say the least a triumphant Church. This will be the true Church and before this, the Church will take her rightful place. This book shows how the church can be a healthy one and all its members can function in the way and manner they should function. As you read this book you will discover that a healthy church will grow naturally without struggle or any inhibition. I have no doubt that this book is needed in our day as we see the imminent return of our King Jesus Christ.

Rev Azuka Ogbolumani
Chapel of Christ our Light
University of Lagos

The time to show the difference between the Church and the world is now! This is the time that God will make up His jewels and put a difference between those who serve Him and those who do not serve Him. This book is very timely and should be read earnestly. Isaac Arikawe has opened up himself to receive these revelations from the Holy Spirit and I recommend that every believer should read this book and apply the teachings to their lives and ministries.

Dr, Chika Ole Kalu
Optometrist, Vital Vision Eye,
Ikeja, Lagos.

I see this book, The True Church as a manual for the working revelation that will equip the Church to fulfill her kingdom mandate on the earth. Isaac Arikawe vividly clarifies the accurate paradigm of the true Church and emphasizes God's agenda, which includes perfecting and maturing the saints and the intimacy with God. I am convinced that if the present Church will build on this foundation, which is Christ, then the whole earth will be filled with God's glory.

Tayo Ladejo
Senior Pastor,
The Governing Church, Ikoyi, Lagos.

I will start by saying that one of the major problems of the church today is that we seek after so much information while neglecting the place of revelation. The church of Jesus Christ was given birth to by revelation and she can only fulfill her mandate on earth by revelation. I hereby call upon whosoever desires to walk with God and is ready to go the extra mile to take time to read this book. And as for the author, I'm not surprised at what God is doing through him. His works in certain parts of Ondo State, Nigeria amongst the churches during the '90s are still speaking till date!

Niyi Sipasi
Pastor, RCCG, Okitipupa, Ondo State.

Even at 20, a man is said to be old if he has stopped reading! The discipline to carefully read through this piece is all that is needed for the contents to be fully absorbed and destiny maximized. Furthermore, since the height and strength of a building are determined by its foundation, The True Church" is the long awaited book that returns individuals who care to diligently study it, back to the foundation of Christendom. Remember that even the righteous is helpless, lacks dignity and honour when the foundation is destroyed. I appreciate the servant of God for this book at a time like this. God bless you.

Dr. Akeremale A. Stephen
Lagos University Teaching Hospital (LUTH)
Lagos

In The True Church, Isaac Arikawe explains the concept of "Church" (Ekklesia) in a manner that depicts her true purpose. He also emphasizes the need for interdependence in the church and the need to be united as a body. He explains that disconnection is equal to death. I join him to urge the church together so we can subdue the only enemy of God. Let all the leaders of the body re-focus on the only assignment, we have to "cultivate the earth." The Church is the role model with the mandate to showcase the glory of our King on earth. Let us rise up and shine as the light that we are. This is a must read for the true believer who wants to please our King.

Funmi Johnson
Author, The Secret Black Book of Wealth.

The Bible says that if the foundations be destroyed, what shall the righteous do? (Psalm 11:3) The word "Church" today has come to mean a lot of things to a lot of people. That the church is dead or alive today is a consequence of the fundamental, foundational belief of the propagators and followers of "The Church". Isaac

Arikawe's "The Dead Living Church" and "The True Church" take us to the origins of the concept and purpose of the church and its relevance to our existence to help us gain understanding of God's will for His Church. You will find this series most revealing.

Emeka Nwako
Pastor-in-charge, RCCG,
Adonai Parish, Area 70,s
Lagos Province 12

In ministry, there are those who are called of God and there are also those who call themselves. The fact, however, is that the difference between them is usually clear. Pastor Isaac Arikawe is called with a clear apostolic mandate to set in order the things that are wanting in the body of Christ. This truth is exemplified in the message of this book. This masterpiece in your hand is loaded with the priceless truth of all ages and also with the power of endless life. As you read a line, you will want to read more. If you are sure you are going somewhere as a believer and you are tired of religion, this book is for you!

Sola Iwaeni
Senior Pastor,
Positive Impact Christian Centre, Lagos

The paradoxical exactitude which is comprehensively explained by Isaac Arikawe in his books, The Dead-Living Church and The True

Church cannot be over-emphasized. It explains the core essence of most church people today. The messages of the books are basically a clarion call for those who have been enmeshed in religious activities without any spiritual productivity to turn a new leaf. Having gone through the books, I can gladly recommend it to anyone who is a true seeker of truth. The explanation of the etymology of the word "Church" gives the reader a platform of better understanding of the concept. Also, the category of our local assemblies today, as seen in the Book of Revelation sets a platform for self-examination for those who think godliness is gain. In all, these books, without doubt would set you at the cutting edge of reformation, revolution and revival. These are must-read books for pastors and parishioners, ministers and members of local assemblies and for those who have been called into the ministry.

Wale Odeniyi
Author, The Kingdom Life
& The Prayer Life Books

The time has come for the true Church to be separated from the false one. This is a time of separation of the wheat from the chaff. The Lord is raising His standards of who the true Church should be as the frequency of His operation on earth increases. In these last days, clarity of sight is coming into the eyes of His prophetic saints to discern the activities within the global church.

The author has done a great job in this book. I recommend it to all who desire to understand the purpose and the power of the true Church.

Tony Azonuche
President, Joshua Generation
CEO, DIVTECH Communications.

Appreciation

To God be the glory for this great work of grace.

Special thanks to my parents: Mr. & Mrs. Adesola Arikawe and my siblings. You are the best and I love you all for your support and your love. Pastor & Mrs. David Adeoye, I place a high premium on our relationship. Pastor and Mrs. Sola Iwaeni, you are a great gift to my life. Thanks for not giving up on me.

Wale Odeniyi, your efforts in proofreading this book cannot be forgotten, you are wonderful. To all my many friends all over the world that I couldn't mention - you are all important to my life.

I also appreciate Pastor Ndukuba of the MFM Church who took the time to do the final editing of these books.

A special thanks to Dr. D.K Olukoya for your special interest, advice and support in bringing this publication to reality. You are God- sent and your kind of heart for the kingdom is rare. May God continue to uphold you.

To my wife, my treasure, the best thing that has ever happened to me after my salvation, you are indeed God-sent. Thank you for being so patient in making all the necessary corrections. Life without you would have been meaningless. Love you so much.

Author's Note

There is nothing a man can receive if it has not been released to him from heaven. It is out of the volume from which a man has received that he can give out. This is a release from Heaven for this generation.

This book is a revelation from God. I decided to end the first part, The Dead-Living Church because of the large volume. As the Spirit of God began to download more truths into my heart, when I got to chapter three, the Holy Spirit changed the tone of the writing and I began to write in a higher frequency totally different from the pattern I was used to in the earlier chapters. As I began to write chapter five, the spirit of the Lord gave me a new title different from what I originally had in mind, that is The Dead- Living Church, volume two to The True Church. Indeed, this title is accurate, as you will soon confirm during the course of reading this book. It is highly explicable and revelational. It is not an intellectual piece of writing, but a creation of the Spirit of God. I believe God has something in mind to correct in our generation so that we can lay a good foundation for the ones to come. You will definitely thank God that this book came your way. You are forever blessed.

Isaac Arikawe K

Introduction

Jesus replied, "You are blessed, Simon, son of John, because My Father in heaven has revealed this to you. You did not learn this from any human being. Now I say to you that you are Peter (which means 'rock'), and upon this rock I will build my Church, and all the power of hell will not conquer it.

Matthew 16:17-18

"He did this to present her to Himself a glorious church without a spot or wrinkle or any other blemish. Instead, she will be holy and without fault."

Ephesians 5:27

This book reveals the distinguishing identity traits of the true church, its positioning, working, operations and functionality. It is a continuation of the first volume- The Dead-Living Church. The first book reveals the concept that Jesus had in mind when he said to Pete; "Now I say to you that you are Peter (which means rock) and upon this I will build my church, and all the power of hell (gates of Hades) will not conquer it" (Mathew 16:18).

The True Church reveals what traits should be looked for in any living or true church. There is a lot of glitz, glamour and competition in the church today and this has made people more confused in our generation. They find it very difficult to separate the true church from the Synagogue of Satan. The church as a spiritual entity has its earthly roles and responsibilities.

The full multi-dimensional manifestation of the true church is carefully and comprehensively explained in this book.

The purpose of the church can never be separated from her identity. This means that if the true identify of a church is lost, that church is dead. The truth is that since the third century the church has gotten it wrong and its state today is a serious concern of heaven. I believe this book will serve as a corrective measure and a source of great change in the operations of the church on earth. I equally believe that it will align men to the true purpose of God, and men would be ready to allow God take His place in the midst of the church. My earnest expectation is that at the end, the church would fulfill her earthly purpose, while preparing for the return of the King.

This book is concluded with prophecies about what is about to take place. Make up your mind for total transformation that will come your way and ministry as you allow the Holy Spirit to guide you in studying the rich and powerful truths revealed in this book. May this work produce a testimony in your life.

Isaac Arikawe K.

Chapter One

The Birth of The Promised Church

"The greatness of a man of God is not measured by the number of thousands that are answerable to him, but by the number of thousands he is serving with his life."

"For the son man came not to be served, but to serve others and to give his life as a ransom for many"

Matthew 20:28

Church is the English translation of the Greek word, Ekklesia. Ekklesia has different shades of meaning. In ancient Greece, the citizens could relate with the term ekklesia, because they had constituted authority or the parliament, being the highest body that handled knotty and notorious issues of that period. See Acts 19:32, 39. Ekklesia means to call out of, or from, that is, an assembly gathered out of a multitude; viz. the Church of God; the congregation collected by God and devoted to his service. The Church of Christ: the whole company of Christians wherever found; because, by the preaching of the Gospel, they are called out of the spirit and maxims of the world, to live according to the precepts of Christ.

Therefore, Jesus understood the meaning of ekklesia; it functions as a lawful assembly, one legally wonder some people thought that Jesus was coming for a political appointment, like the King the of Jews.

Also, ekklesia does not in any form refer to a building or a structure made with hands, but a congregation of people, called out for a specific task, such as delegates, parliament, senate, council or a board of directors.

Therefore, our denominational local assemblies or churches are not supposed to be independent assemblies as it is being practiced today, but interdependent. This means that though each assembly exists with its distinct and different flavour / assignment, yet they function like a committee in charge of a particular issue within a central Assembly or Senate, which is the Body of Christ. Today, many have got drunk with personal vision or selfish ambition (called committee/denominational assembly) and forgotten the central vision, which is the Kingdom and the King that called us into the assembly of the "called out", the Church.

THE CHURCH OF JESUS CHRIST

It is obvious that the scope and the workings of Jesus' promised Church is far beyond human comprehension and larger in dimension than what the Greeks were used to in terms of the word, ekklesia.

In Acts chapter one, Jesus was emphatic in His command to the disciples not to leave Jerusalem until the Father sends them the Gift, i.e. the Holy Spirit, that He promised. "Though John baptized with water, but in just a few days you will be baptized with the Holy Spirit" (Acts 1:5).

This also reveals that the software that built up the Church of Jesus Christ are far beyond human imagination. It was not a product of the physical senses, but of the Spirit of God. The book of Acts in chapter two reveals the workings and deeds of the Spirit, when about 120 believers were meeting together in the house.

"On the day of Pentecost all the believers were meeting together in one place. Suddenly, there was a sound from heaven like the roaring of a mighty windstorm, and it filled the house where they were sitting. Then, what looked like flames or tongues of fire appeared and settled on each of them. And everyone present was filled with the Holy Spirit and began speaking in other languages as the Holy Spirit gave them this ability" (Acts 2:1-4).

We can see from the scriptures above that Jesus did not specify a particular house for them to gather together in Jerusalem. The bottom line was that they were gathered unto the Lord. The Bible says they (believers) were meeting together in one place. If emphasis on the place (building) of the meeting was critical, it would have been mentioned.

Secondly, the sound from heaven like the roaring of the mighty windstorm that filled the house was not dependent on the physical building. It happened because the believers were gathered in obedience to the Lord's command. Therefore, if they had gathered somewhere else, the same experience would still have occurred.

Thirdly, the Scriptures recorded in verse four, "that everyone present was filled with the Holy Spirit and began speaking in other languages." This expresses the fact that it was not the building that was filled with the Spirit but the yielded vessels. The truth is this: the Spirit of God does not reside in any building; no matter how nice and sacred it may be to man, His Spirit resides in people who have made themselves available and ready for the experience. The experience is also not a by-product of religious practices.

I find it baffling today, seeing men of God putting pressure on the people in a bid to amass properties for use as worship centers. However, they have placed less emphasis on the condition of dying men who come to worship religiously in that facility. I don't have a problem with a local assembly acquiring a befitting modern structure, fully equipped for worship, but it should not be at the expense of dead-living men who appear to have a form of godliness but deny the power of God.

I have seen in many places of worship that men are no longer interested in the undiluted word of God and commitment to fellowship and true worship has depreciated. However, in these places they have perfected the art of raising money at all cost to build personal empires in the name of churches. These churches have misplaced their priorities. Eventually, the fire will destroy all structures of falsehood, but the structure Jesus was talking about is one built without human hands. I see many local assemblies (denominations) today competing on the basis of the buildings, which they are using for worship. This is foolishness and a distraction of the devil.

This scenario was what Jesus had in mind when He addressed the Pharisees: "What sorrow awaits you teachers of religious law and you Pharisees? Hypocrites! For you are like white washed tombs- beautiful on the outside but filled on the inside with dead people's bones and all sorts of impurity" (Matthew 23:27). Beloved, I don't know how you feel about this scripture, the truth is that God is not interested in many of the religious activities we are spending much of our time, money and other resources. It is all about the people. They are not the reason for everything He promised. How will you feel when everything you have labored and toiled for decades is rejected? Reason: your pattern and technology is absolutely different from those of the designer Jesus. How long have you gone in the wrong direction that you are feeling bad to turn around?

Pause and take a decision that will give your work eternal value today, or else you will receive the word "Depart from me, I never knew you, you workers of iniquity." (Matthew 7:23)

You can only be rewarded for building to His specification. I pray that your labour shall not be in vain.

Chapter Two

The Church: A Spiritual Entity

The greatest thing that can happen to a man is not to be connected to the world- wide web (www) but to the source of life.

"Remain in me, and I will remain in you. For a branch cannot produce fruit if it is severed from the vine, and you cannot be fruitful unless you remain in me"

John 15:4

The emergence of the Church was not by human calculations, but by the power of the Holy Spirit. The Bible records that the believers were not so different from the other Jews and Gentiles. The distinguishing factor was that they abandoned everything to follow Jesus. It was this decision that made them followers of Jesus. However, they did not become the Church until the experience of the Holy Spirit in the house where they all gathered.

"Suddenly, there was a sound from heaven like the roaring of a mighty windstorm, and it filled the house where they were setting. Then, what looked like flames or tongues of fire appeared and settled on each of them. And everyone present was filled with the Holy Spirit and began speaking in other languages, as the Holy Spirit gave them this ability" Acts 2:2-4

CRITICAL SUCCESS FACTORS FROM THE PASSAGE:

Decoding the sound from heaven is not a function of any sophisticated gadget but the right positioning of the heart and ears in the direction of God's leading.

There are sounds in the air - frequencies even right where you are but you can only pick up or hear them if you are connected to a certain network provider and that you are with your decoder or the mobile phone. Acts 2:2 says "suddenly, there was a sound from heaven..., and filled the house they were sitting". This sound did not fill the city of Jerusalem, where prominent people had gathered for a worldwide conference, but the house where the disciples were assembled.

God's presence is not limited to functioning in a particular location; all He needs is a right atmosphere to operate.

This suggests to me that even those in the toilet in the same house where they were gathered also experienced the same impartation. Little wonder, Jesus Himself told a Samaritan woman who was tribal-centric and conscious of a worship location in the book of John, Chapter 4: "Believe me, dear woman, the time is coming when it will no longer matter whether you worship the father on this mountain or in Jerusalem... But the time is coming- indeed, it's here now when true worshippers will worship the father in the spirit and in truth. The father is looking for those who will worship him that way." (John4:21, 24). Therefore, it doesn't matter where you go to receive a call or a signal, if you are not connected, it is just a waste of time. God cannot be circumscribed to a geographical location. All you need is to develop your ability and capacity to receive from Him. It is a sanctified man that makes a sanctuary sacred. It is not the reverse.

The book of Acts 2 confirms this assertion in verse 3: "Then, what looked like flames or tongues of fire appeared and settled on each of them." That which looked like flames or tongues of fire that appeared did not settle on any part of the house where they gathered; not even where Peter, the General Overseer, was seated, but on each individual who was in His presence, in obedience to the Master's words.

Friends, we must kick religion out of our system. Haven't you realized that the rain and the dew that fall from heaven do not recognize or separate a small tree from the little grass of the field? It would follow then that in a true church setting (local assembly), every member (followers and the leaders) must be able to have a personal experience or encounter with the Holy Spirit. There is no longer a place for the Holy of Holies or the Most Holy Place; no more boundaries and limitations in accessing the presence of God. Everyone can approach God through the singular sacrifice of His Son, Jesus Christ, and by the enabling power of the Holy Spirit.

"For Christ himself has brought peace to us. He united Jews and Gentiles into one people when, in his own body on the cross, he broke down the wall of hostility (partition /barrier) that separated us." Ephesians 2:14

Beloved, one of the symptoms of a dead Church is having thousands of people, i.e., followers, running around the leader for an absolute prophetic direction for their lives. A true shepherd is expected to teach, nourish and disciple men to a level of maturity where they can hear God for themselves like Samuel. Many spiritual heads enjoy and crave to see people flocking round them, queuing to see them, lording over the Church of Jesus Christ. They have invariably taken over the place of God in their lives; such men have succeeded in digging graves for their future.

Why don't you pause and check your inner motives today and be sincere with yourself? Apostle Paul calls us to self-examination through which we can avert condemnation, provided there is true repentance.

There can never be a true church without the infilling of the Holy Spirit on the Congregation as an evidence

The Bible records in Acts 2 verse 4: "And everyone present was filled with the Holy Spirit and began speaking in other languages." It is the ministry of the Holy Spirit that activates and confirms a Church. As a matter of fact, every activity of an assembly must be Holy Spirit inspired and driven. The holy Spirit is God in us; when He comes into a believer; he becomes God's carrier on earth. It means that God now resides in you. This should be a craving and a yearning of every believer. It makes your walk and work with God smooth, without frustration. I am not saying that with the Holy Spirit there would not be challenges. They will definitely come. However, their presence helps us to build our faith into maturity. In the midst of all the challenges you will not lose the peace of God, His righteousness and the Joy of Holy Ghost. You will be able to differentiate an attack of the devil from the trials of faith, which are expected to build us to the next level of our walk with God.

Jesus expatiated on the work of the Holy Spirit and the need to have this life changing experience to his disciples in John 14: 15-17: "if you love me, obey my Commandments. And I will ask the father, and he will give you another Advocate (Comforter/counselor), who will never leave you. He is the Holy Spirit, who leads into all truth. The world cannot receive him, because it isn't looking for him and doesn't recognize him. But you know him, because he lives with you now and later will be in you". Jesus went on to assert in John 16: 7: "Also but in fact, it is best for you that I go away, because if I don't the Advocate (Comforter/counselor) won't come. If I do go away, then I will send him to you".

THE MAJOR WORK OF HOLY SPIRIT WITHIN THE CHURCH

"He convicts the world of its sin, and of God, righteousness, and of the coming Judgment." John 16:8

With the help of the Holy Spirit, it becomes very easy to live above sin. Whenever you want to say or do something wrong, He quickly reminds you and gives you the enablement to live up to God's standard of righteousness and consequently opens your eyes to the consequences that follow. Therefore, every believer as a member of God's body, must strive to rely on the Holy Spirit on a daily basis. We must learn from the mistake of Ananias and Sapphira who fell after they had partaken in the apostolic grace. They hardened their hearts at the correction of the Holy Spirit, who must have warned them of the spirit of mammon; greed, lying and selfishness, yet they disobeyed. They also wanted to bring their polluted spirit to defile the body of Christ, the apostolic team, but Peter, a man full of the spirit of discernment, could smell deception in the air. He responded in Acts 5:3:"Ananias, why have you let Satan fill your heart? You lied to the Holy Spirit, and you kept some of the money for yourself. The property was yours to sell or not sell, as you wished. How could you do a thing like this? You weren't lying to us, but to God." We can see from the next verse that Ananias fell down and died with his wife who also refused to repent.

The same spirit has crept into the Church today. From the pulpit to the pew, men are taking the grace of God for granted, to commit all sorts of atrocities, just because the Ananias experience is no longer common. The truth is that churches are becoming dead and the Holy Spirit is no longer in His place in the Church.

The second work of the Holy Spirit is revealed in John 16:13: "When the spirit of truth comes, he will guide you into all truth. He will not speak on his own, but will tell you what he has heard. He will tell you about the future."

It is extremely impossible to walk in an accurate truth without the aid of the Holy Spirit. Jesus says in John 14:6: "I am the way, the truth and the life. No one can come to the father except through me." And He further attested to this fact in John 14:17: "He is the Holy Spirit, who leads into all truth..." Living a moral life does not equate with a truthful life. A moralist operates from a soulish realm while the truthful person is a man that has submitted his life to Jesus Christ. He said, "I am the way, the truth and the life." This is something beyond what the human brain can comprehend. Here, I am not talking about truthfulness from the point of not telling lies, but coming into the truth that Jesus is the Lord and Saviour, Who died for your sins so that you might be free forever. This is one of the truths that the devil has hidden from you in order to prevent you from living an accurate life that will bring glory to God.

The third work of the Holy Spirit is that "He will bring me glory by telling you whatever he receives from me. All that belongs to the father is mine; this is why I said, "The Spirit will tell you whatever he receives from me." John 16:14-15

The summary of this third function is twofold: He enables you to bring glory to God via your life style. He reveals the mind of Jesus to you. What is the purpose of your living as a child of God? If you can't hear, from Him, you are a dead-living person. This is one of the works of the Holy Spirit in the life of a believer and by so doing, He brings glory to Jesus. This experience of hearing God speak to you clearly and unambiguous shouldn't be the exclusive of the pastors or the ministry heads, but it should be for everyone. Anything else simply means that this is a congregation of the dead.

THE PHILOSOPHY BEHIND JESUS' CHURCH

The philosophy of any subject matter reveals the beliefs, the attitude, the purpose or its raison d'être, i.e., the reason for being. What is the ideology behind Jesus establishing His own church? First He declared His intention of building His own class of church, and then He made the content, capacity, ability, her placement and positioning on earth known. Mathew 16:17-1 says: "Jesus replied, you are blessed, Simon, son of John because my father in heaven has revealed this to you, you did not learn this from any human being. Now I say to you that you are Peter (which means rock) and upon this rock I will build my church, and the powers of the hell will not conquer it. And I will give you the keys of the Kingdom of Heaven. Whatever you permit on earth will be permitted in heaven."

In the process of searching for the philosophy behind the church that Jesus built, the following are the keys we would need to note:

1. The Greek meaning of the word "church".

The term CHURCH in Greek, ekklesia, occurs for the first time in Matthew 16:18. The word simply means an assembly or congregation, the nature of which is to be understood from connecting circumstances. Jesus used this word to express His own mind and technology. The word was frequently used to describe an assembly of citizens of a Greek city. Also in Acts 19:32-39, the

Hebrew term, "qahal" refers to an "assembly". In our contemporary society, it would be described as a senate or parliament, which is a strong, formidable, constituted authority with a vested power to operate. Jesus declares further that His proposed Church will not be conquered by all the powers of hell.

We shouldn't forget that in the beginning, it was one of these powers of hell that conquered Adam and Eve. From there, they lost the first dominion mandate to the devil (Gen 1:26). So, Jesus saw the need to raise competent saints (the church) that would live above sin and subdue the powers of hell. Therefore, at Pentecost, He gave a higher and incontrovertible power to the disciples as promised.

Jesus also promised to give the keys of the kingdom to this very church, which symbolizes the highest authority on the planet earth, to the extent that whatsoever this brand of church binds on earth, the heavens will rubber stamp it, and even the power to forgive sins has been bestowed on the church. If this church should be exactly as promised by the originator, it would be an extension of heaven on earth. By so doing, every government of the earth comes to it for instructions because such a set of people known as the church can end the regime of such governments can stop the sun from appearing, and the rain from falling on the land, thereby subjecting people to the lordship of Jesus. I mean an ekklesia that is vested with indescribable power and authority. Joshua, the right hand man of Moses, was keyed into this realm when he interrupted the chronological order of time. He commanded the sun to stand still and it obeyed. This was also what Elijah did by interrupting the national economy of Israel during the reign of King Ahab, by grinding the agricultural business, which was their main source of income, to zero until they bowed before the true and living God.

On this premise, we can come to the conclusion that the philosophy behind Jesus' call for building of His own Church, is to raise up competent saints who will make life miserable for the devil and his agents and bring man back to the apogee of dominion, greater than the state of Adam before the fall. Romans 5:17 says: "For the sin of this one man, Adam caused death to rule over many. But even greater is God's wonderful grace and his gift of righteousness, for all who receive it will live in triumph over sin and through this one man Jesus Christ." 1 Corinthians 15:45 also tells us: "The first man, Adam, became a living person (soul) but the last Adam that is, Christ is a life giving spirit."

You can see clearly from the scriptures above that the Church Jesus built was of higher capacity, potency and accuracy than the first one at the Garden of Eden before the fall. We should ask ourselves at this juncture: where is the church Jesus intentionally and purposefully built? What is the quality of its impact in "our world" as a church? Can we boldly say that the gates /powers of hell are not prevailing over our system again? How have we managed the power and authority bequeathed to us as a church? If these questions cannot be answered correctly, it means the church, "assembly of the called out" we belong to, is dead and merely existing.

In conclusion, the church is a spiritual entity and not just a human organization that can be managed by the whims and caprices of men or theological research. No! It can only be by the Spirit. As far as I am concerned, the highest insult or derogative remark anyone can hurl at me in the name of compliment is to tell me that I am very spiritual. I have seen a lot of people feel very cool based on this compliment, "you are very spiritual". The import of this assertion to me is that you are carnal and sensual, but once in a while you tune in to the Holy Ghost frequency.

What the devil is trying to do is to water down my identity. We are fundamentally spirit beings; so there is nothing like I am spiritual. For a long time, I did not reply religious men who in the name of Christianity ask me, "Bro, how is your Christian life?" My reason is not far-fetched; I don't have two lives. I have only one life. That question is a hypocritical question. As a child of God, one should have and live only one life, which Jesus has given to us. Your "other lives" have been nailed to the cross. Therefore, at all times, in the market place, and in your place of work, at school, at home or in the church, we should be conscious of only one life.

Chapter Three

The Church: The Body of Christ

"I don't regard a man to be a millionaire until his pockets have benefited millions of lives for better."

"And I have been a constant example of how you can help those in need by working hard. You should remember the words of the Lord Jesus, it is more blessed to give than to receive"

Acts 20:35

The Oxford Advanced Learners' Dictionary defines "body" as follows: The whole physical structure of a human being or an animal: the main part of a body not including the head. A group of people who work or act together, often for an official purpose, or who are connected in some other way.

Apostle Paul had a great revelation about the bodily relationship between Christ and Church, which is indicative of our positioning and placement as the church of Jesus Christ. As the Spirit of God will help us, we shall be looking into this analysis to see clearly the mind of the Father.

Apostle Paul in his first letter to the Corinthians aptly paints the true picture of the modus operandi of the body system.

"The human body has many parts, but the many parts make up one whole body. So it is with the body of Christ. Some of us are Jews, some are Gentiles, some are slaves and some are free. But we have all been baptized into one body by one spirit and we share from the same Spirit. Yes, the body has many different parts, not just one part. If the foot says, "I am not a part of the body because I am not a hand" that does not make it any less a part of the body. And if the ear says, "I am not part of the body because I am not an eye", would that make it any less a part of the body? If the whole body were an eye how would you hear? Or if your whole body were an ear, how would you smell anything? But our bodies have many parts and God put each part just where he wants it. How strange a body would be if it had only one part! Yes, there are many parts, but only one body. The eyes can never say to the hand, "I don't need you". The head can't say to the feet, "I don't need you". In fact, some parts of the body that seem weakest and least important are actually the most necessary. And the parts we regard as less honorable are those we clothe with the greatest care. So we carefully protect those parts that should not be seen, while the more honorable parts do not require this special care. So God has put the body together such that extra honor and care are given to those parts that have less dignity. This makes for harmony among the members, so that all the members care for each other. If one part suffers, all the parts suffer with it, and if one part is honored, all the parts are glad. All of you together are Christ's body, and each of you is a part of it. (1 Corinthians 12: 12-26).

A complete being can be categorized into two main parts: the head and the entire body. We shall consciously look at each category. Kindly, permit me to start with the body. The diagram below shall be used to highlight the salient points for clarity and a thorough comprehension.

A COMPLETE BEING

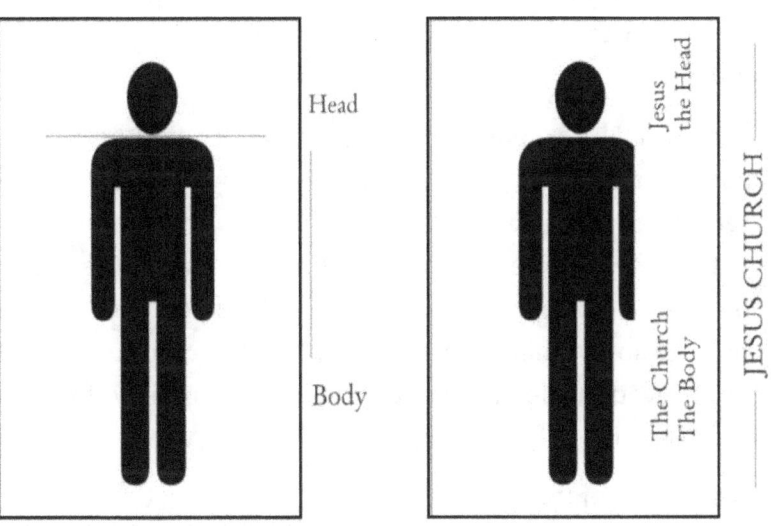

ONE BODY, MANY PARTS

The writing of this book arose out of a divine instruction and a long time burden for the Church of Jesus Christ. God has taken me through many denominations and local assemblies; I have met different ministers and church leaders. I have also worked with these people voluntarily with a view to helping them realize their vision and the work placed a great burden and challenge on me.

It is disturbing to note from my personal discovery and relationship with these assemblies that a majority of these people does not understand the concept of Jesus church and the principles behind the Body of Christ, one body with many parts. This is why the church of Jesus Christ is very weak and inefficient. Many of the so-called visionary leaders have succeeded in hijacking the church from Jesus. They have cornered and converted the Church of Jesus to their personal property, an extension of their business enterprise. Thus, they are building through their vain ambition a great empire for themselves. This trend, which has become quite pervasive today, is what worries me. However, the only thing I resolved to do is to pray and I believe this book in your hand is an answer to prayers.

Even, if I have something to say, most of our fathers in the Lord and friends are not accessible. They have built walls around themselves and ego has done so much to them that they don't relate with such men like us who have no name. They cannot sit down and believe God would use such "men like this" to speak to them. Although there are still few who have died to self and have not believed the lie of the devil, the sincere humility that such rare men exude is really humbling.

The crux of the matter is that for a very long time now, a lot of people have pioneered their own establishments or enterprises in the name of the Lord. They have started their "own church" outside the Master's blueprint. Some have actually been called God, but are deceived along the way while others call themselves to ministry for personal ambition and aggrandizement. My consolation is this: God knows the intent of every man's heart.

Every operation of the Father, the Son and Holy Spirit, has demonstrated to us that unity is a sine qua non, an absolute necessity. Trinity refers to three that are in unity. So if the components that make up the head are in unity, why should the body be divided? God did not give humanity many sacrifices, one for each person, but a singular price for all mankind. He paid one major sacrifice to unite the body.

Therefore, as the physical body comprises many parts like shoulders, arms, hands, fingers, waist, hips, thighs, knees, heels, feet, ankles, navel, etc., so do we all together make up a body, the body of Christ. It comprises different entities and personalities, individuals, local assemblies and the entire global church which you and I are part of and are expected to be one. We would use these diagrams again for more explanations.

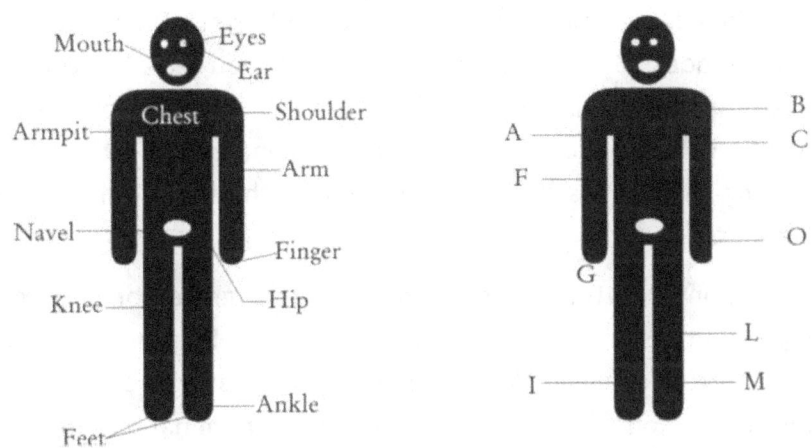

From the above diagrams, most parts are labeled with a name or an alphabet as the case may be. As for the body of Jesus Christ, which is the church, every part labeled each alphabet refers to each of us or each local assembly (the churches) that form the entire church, which is the complete assembly.

Let's assume that alphabets A and B are local assemblies within the same country while alphabets L and M are assemblies in another country. Though each group is far from the other and are not physically in touch, they are connected together by the same veins, tissues and blood. Just imagine if L and M, parts of the body demand to be on their own, and see themselves as separate entities, how would they get their supply of blood and nutrients? It means our living is dependent on the same source, which connects us together.

We shouldn't allow culture, race, ethnicity, tribe, language or human classification; first world countries, second world countries or third world, to divide us. These classifications and stratifications are not of the Kingdom - Zion, but a satanic agenda propagated by the Babylonian system to cause a division within the body. All these factors must be deleted from our spirit being if we are going to function as a whole body.

Beloved, the amount of grace, favor and revelation you may be carrying doesn't matter as long as it makes you feel that you are more important than others. It doesn't matter how blossoming and beautiful the edifice may look to mere men; that which you are building without a sense of connectivity with others will produce deadness.

This implies that there is no available grace for the self-dependent assembly, but the interdependent will receive a deluge of grace from heaven. We need one another to survive and to fulfill our purpose on earth. The era of being a denomination-bound in your heart and not seeing, brethren from other local churches as part of the body is no longer relevant. Have you forgotten that the name of your local assembly will not be mentioned in heaven on the day of reckoning, but the roll call of the redeemed and transformed will be read out?

DISCONNECTION EQUALS DEATH

A proverb says that a stream that forgets its source would quickly dry up. So is every life that is cut off from the mainstream; it will eventually experience death. Let's just imagine again that Brother I in the diagram above and ministry C and D are complaining about the wrong behavior of the other parts and gradually withdraw themselves from the entire body. The truth is that they won't survive it.

This great attack on the body of Christ has gone so deep that even in the same local assembly, people are worshiping with malice, hatred, uncaring attitude, intimidation, oppression, segregation and many factions. Some pastors or spiritual heads have their own cabals, not by functions, but by reason of personal benefits. There is no more hope for the widows, fatherless and less privileged. The voice of the poor man is silenced. This can never be a true picture of the body of Christ.

Many of our operations can be likened to the workings of the Pharisees and the religious leaders, who lived by selfishness and see with myopic eyes instead of the King's vision. Hypocritical men can never please God. In fact, Jesus exposed their shenanigans and cursed them. (See Matthew 23:1 to end). You may be tempted to ask: "why did Jesus curse them? There was no genuine service from their hearts to bless humanity, but for their self-aggrandizements and personal gains."

Let us see Apostle Paul's admonition against division in the church: I appeal to you, dear brothers and sisters, by the authority of our lord Jesus Christ, to live in harmony with each other. Let there be no divisions in the church. Rather, be of one mind, united in thought and purpose.

For some members of Chloe's household have told me about your quarrels, my dear brothers and sisters. Some of you are

saying, "I am a follower of Paul. Others are saying, "I follow Apollos", or "I follow Peter, "or I follow only Christ". Has Christ been divided into factions? Was I, Paul crucified for you? Were any of you baptized in the name of Paul? Of course not! I thank God that I did not baptize any of you except Crispus and Gaius. For now, no one can say they were baptized in my name"
1 Corinthians 1: 10-15

Beloved, we need to key into the apostolic spirit, which Paul carried; one, which only centred on the purpose of God and His will alone. Imagine being in the shoes of Paul, where congregations are confused and quarrelling, grading and placing preachers as first class and second class. Paul was an orator, and he could have gathered the people that preferred him to Apollos and encouraged them by giving them positions, a trend which is very common today in our assemblies, local churches and ministries. He could as well have thought of opening another branch of Apostle Paul's ministry and ended up dividing the first church, gather a people to himself, and build a personal empire in the name of ministry. Beloved, I have this word of prophecy from the Lord: every such ministry of "me", "myself" and "I" will collapse not too long from now because their origins and foundations are faulty, and the church of Christ must not die.

The best thing we can do to ourselves is not to run a self-imposed target that has no divine backing and eternal value. Even if your building process is slow, God knows your ability. He will help you, but you must have a genuine reason for everything you do.

I have said to myself, if He that called me into this ministry cannot feed me, I'd prefer dying on my way to fulfilling His will then live by manipulation. Neither am I ready to worship any man for what I will eat or for a position. God that has called me; who employed me is much more capable to pay me. What is needed is faithfulness to our individual calling and assignments.

COVENANT RELATIONSHIP AND COMMUNITY LIVING WITHIN THE BODY

A covenant is a sealed agreement between two or more persons or organizations. An example is a marriage covenant; in this case a lady and a man come together to sign a statement in the presence of God that they shall live together till death do them part.

The term, community could mean a particular people living together, a group of people who share the same religion, race, job, culture, etc., a very strong feeling of sharing things and belonging to a group.

The blood of Jesus seals the church as a body of Christ, and we are yoked together by a communal spirit which is the purpose and the will of God. Why then are we behaving as if we did not have anything in common?

I would like to dwell more on the local assembly, church or denominations. We are disappointing God; only very few are making God happy. Every local assembly should be a family with a community spirit where true love abounds. It shouldn't be a place where men come to show off their best belongings, cars, clothing, etc. It is supposed to be a house of encouragement, sharing the joy and burden of each other, a place of refreshing, a place of speaking the truth in love to one another without creating hurt, and a place of true intercession for the brethren.

For a very long time, I didn't like brethren calling me "brother Arikawe" or "brother Isaac". Why? I discovered that a lot of believers didn't understand the term the way it was used in the church. The early church used this term, "brother" to mean someone of the same lineage that is, one of the closest relations one can have. Naturally, I love my siblings; I can't stand to see anyone of them suffer. Therefore, in calling ourselves "brother or sister", there is a weight attached to it as members of the body of Christ. So, I don't like all the hypocrisy and religious "brother this and sister that", where there is no genuine display of love, filial affection and concern for the other person's welfare as it should be.

Ask yourself: "How many people have I helped with my position in the marketplace, my resources, my advice or my influence, generally? The truth is that it doesn't matter how much we are praying for everybody's breakthrough, every part of the body can't have the same size and functions. God created all. Why don't you decide to bring joy to Jesus' heart today by changing the way you have been handling the body. Seeing everybody within your assembly should be very important to you. Take time daily to reflect on the welfare and lifestyles of members of this family, the body of Christ, in genuine concern. Start from your own local assembly.

We would not be able to silence our enemy until we are united in the spirit and live as a community. There is strength and safety in number. Remember, the greatness of a man of God is not determined by the number of thousands that serve him, but the number of thousands that he is serving.

In chapter 3 of the Gospel according to Mark, Jesus redefines the concept of brotherhood in a bid to re-orientate His followers. "Jesus mother and brothers came to see him. They stood outside and sent word for him to come and talk with them. There was a crowd sitting around Jesus and someone said, "Your mother and brothers are outside asking for you." Jesus replied, "Who is my mother? Who are my brothers? Then he looked at those around him (his disciples) and said, "Look, these are my mother and brothers, anyone who does God's will is my brother and sister and mother." (Mark 3:31-35).

Here you see that mother, brother and sisters are very close members of one's family, but Jesus is saying that the members of the church, the small group you belong to and the universal church, regardless of the physical demarcations and separation, regardless of the color of the skin of members, are also your brethren. In the same vein, Abraham caught the revelation by calling Lot his brother: And Abram said unto Lot, let there be no strife. I pray thee, between me and thee, and between my herdsmen and thy herdsmen; for we are brethren. (Genesis 13:8). Abraham was an uncle to Lot by family relationship, they were not brothers, but by virtue of the position he placed Lot, Abraham considered him as a brother.

A true communal existence creates a bond, a wall of defense, which the enemy cannot attack. This is what the Lord requires from us. This oneness was the strength of the early church: "All the believers were united in heart and mind. And they felt that what they owned was not their own, so they shared everything they had. The apostles testified powerfully to the resurrection of the Lord Jesus, and God's great blessing was upon them all. There were no needy people among them, because those who owned land or houses would sell them and bring the money to the apostles to give to those in need. For instance, there was Joseph, the one the apostles nicknamed Barnabas (which means "Son of Encouragement"). He was from the tribe of Levi and came from the island of Cyprus. He sold a field he owned and brought the money to the apostles. (Acts 4:32-37).

It is my earnest prayer that this grace will return to the church of Jesus even in a higher dimension; where we would not be living for ourselves but for God and only His purpose. Friend, it doesn't matter the amount of money you have in your bank account, "I don't regard a man as a millionaire until his pocket has touched the lives of millions of people." In rounding up this subject, the admonition of Paul to the Corinthian church is pertinent: "if one part suffers, all the parts suffer with it, and if one part is honored, all the parts are glad." (I Corinthians 12:26) I pray for you, that this message will not stand against you in Judgment.

JESUS, THE HEAD OF THE BODY

A body is useless without the head. The head is the structure on top of the body and that's how God designed it. As big as the body may seem, its most sensitive part that determines the collective destiny is the head. Are you talking about the eye, for sight and direction; ears for hearing and knowing the direction, or the mouth for declaring what you've seen and heard? This means that everything the entire body needs to survive and be fulfilled is within the head. The same is true in the spiritual. Little wonder Jesus said in John 14:6: "I am the way, the truth and the life. No one comes to the father except by me."The head provides direction along the way; it receives insights about the truth of God's word and enables us to fulfill our God- given mission and vision in life. The only thing you need in life to make it and establish the purpose of God for your life is to be located in the head.

Paul also uses the analogy of Christ and the Church in a marital relationship to paint a similar picture of Christ as the head of the body: "For the husband is the head of his wife as Christ is the head of the church. He is the savior of his body, the church. As the Church submits to Christ, so you wives should submit to your husbands in everything." (Ephesians 5:22-23.) Hence, for a church to be living, she must submit absolutely to the lordship of Jesus as the head of the body.

In conclusion, let's read what Jesus himself said about our connectivity as a church: "Yes, I am the vine; you are the branches. Those who do not remain in me are thrown away like a useless branch and wither; such branches are gathered into a pile to be burned." (John 15:5).

Many people have attended courses, seminars and training programs on Church growth, finances, etc. The truth is that human ideas can't handle the things of the Spirit. It does not matter the formula you are applying now, except you are connected to the source and allow your help to come only from God and rely on Him absolutely, frustration is inevitable. Friends, you need God more than ever before to survive. Therefore, any attempt to disconnect either from the entire body or from the Head (Jesus) is death. This is why you see men rating local assemblies and churches by world standards. I once heard a pastor introducing his friend as the best pastor of his zone and pastoring the best church. How do you measure the best church? What are the parameters: is it by population, acquired property, or humanly created influence. It is sad that men are using their finite human senses to grade and rate the Church of Jesus according to the traditions of the world; the best bank, best baby consumer product and the rest. There are no best parts in the body; big or small, everyone has its function and purpose.

Chapter Four

The Church: The Bride of Christ

"Many couples stay together without living together. I come to a conclusion that separation goes beyond divorce while relationship goes beyond staying together."

"But I have this complaint against you. You don't love me or each other as you did at first."

Revelations 2:4

I have had my own fair share of weddings, either as a best man, or being on the groom's train or even as a professional wedding planner. In all of my experiences with brides and bridegrooms of different cultures and backgrounds, I can authoritatively say that there was a common feeling and attitude which they displayed and exuded close to their wedding day or during the wedding proper and a few hours after their wedding.

Who then is a bride? The dictionary defines a bride as "a woman on her wedding day, or just before or just after it." Therefore, a bride is not just a name or appellation for every woman to answer. What makes the bride different from another? It is found in her mood, emotional state at this given period, her expectations, and the expectations of the bridegroom and others from her.

I have come to discover that this is one of the most exciting periods in the life of every woman. This is also the very period that demands serious planning, organization and attention to details. Despite the fact that the bride's expectations and reactions towards her wedding day are so much pronounced, this does not change the fact that the bridegroom is also full of his own expectations.

THE BRIDE'S (THE CHURCH) POSITION IN JESUS' LIFE

Let us be glad and rejoice, and let us give honor to him. For the time has come for the wedding feast of the Lamb, and his bride has prepared herself. She has been given the finest of pure white linen to wear". For the fine linen represents the good deeds of God's holy people. (Revelation 19:7-8).

The greatest disaster that can ever happen to a bride is to be disappointed by her would-be husband a few days or hours to the wedding ceremony. May be you don't understand what I'm talking about. On two occasions, I personally witnessed and participated in consoling a bride who came and begged to return her purchased wedding items and another man who did the same because his wife to be had received a gunshot, just a few hours to their wedding. As a manager then, I was overwhelmed by pity and emotion to the extent that I pleaded with my CEO to change the company's policy of "no refund" just because, I could feel and empathize with these aggrieved ones.

There is a world of difference between a wedding and a marriage. A Wedding is a momentary thing while a marriage is a movement, a journey. It requires a longer timing than the short period of waiting.

Secondly, there can be a good wedding without a good marriage. Time is a Revealer of every good marriage. This means that a man could be very happy on his wedding day spend his life regretting the marriage.

It is a thing of joy to have a man who has promised marriage to a lady being committed to the promise, ready to spend the rest of his life with her. What a very hard and costly decision! The state of the church is at a point where she is engaged to a very committed and a sincere lover (Jesus) but she on her part is not ready to keep to the rules of the courtship. The bride, i.e., the Church, is very self-centered. Most men and women who come to do so only for what they can get from Him, not because they care about His own needs. Has it ever occurred to you that the Father and the Son also have pressing needs?

This category of brides is happy that it is secure in its selfish and one-sided relationship with Jesus. At least, they are sure of having him for marriage; self-interest and they end up going out with other bridegrooms. For some people, the truth is that the only time they ever deeply remember Jesus is when the powers, authorities and principalities are about to molest their life and destroy their destiny. Then, they remember Jesus as a reserve, a backup, support and the power of His blood. They also forget that He needs relationship before seeking and thinking about you, but after finding you, and you agreed to be His forever, the grace to be committed is not there any longer.

According to Revelation 19:7, you are like a bride who goes about telling people about her wedding day and making every necessary arrangement for the wedding ceremony, meanwhile the marriage is not a point of concern to her. No wonder in the world today, deceit has become a normal thing, even at the center of the Church.

The truth of the matter is that Jesus can never be deceived. Man looks at the appearance, but Jesus looks straight into the hearts of men. He knows His own and His owner knows him. If you are living hypocritically, make your way right because, when the marriage hour comes, we shall see openly the true brides and the deceptive ones.

Friend, pause for a moment and examine yourself, regardless of the way you paint yourself to people about your false relationship, making people believe that Jesus is the only love of your life, when you know deep inside you that there are other lovers contesting His place in your life. If He calls for the marriage today, will you be a qualified partaker of the feast? Register this in your mind today that your face i.e., eyes service does not move God, but your faithfulness, and the service from the heart. This is the only guarantee that you will get an invitation to the wedding of the Lamb.

THE NECESSARY CONDITIONS FOR THE MARRIAGE

It is not every courtship or engagement that leads to marriage. Sometimes, a lot would have been invested; i.e., emotional, material, financial and time spent together, but at the end it would not work for one reason or the other. At times, one party might get wounded emotionally while the other party feels nothing; but the end determines who will sustain a permanent injury in the course of the broken relationship.

Therefore, it is very possible for a man's mouth to "confess" Jesus as Lord and his heart is working against that purpose. It means that there was no genuine encounter in the first place. Many come to the Lord not just because they truly desire to give their hearts to Him, but because the problems, challenges and the pressure of life have brought them to Him. They go back to their initial philosophy of life after the challenges have disappeared. The Bible says God can never be deceived, whatsoever a man sows he shall also reap. (Galatians 6:7).

In Revelation 19:8, we see that this bride (Church) has been given her wedding gown to prepare for the wedding. "She has been given the finest of pure white linen to wear". For the fine linen represents the good deeds of God's holy people.

What this means is that, Jesus, the bridegroom, has made a promise and hope to marry the bride to the extent that the woman (Church) is already being addressed as a bride. This is telling us that the time is very close for any man to be playing cards with it. This shouldn't be a time when the woman (bride) should be reconsidering any other bridegrooms. It should be a time of sober reflection and attention to detail as she prepares for the bridegroom (Jesus), who will not notify you (the bride) of his appearance for the wedding hour.

Therefore, it doesn't matter how long you have been answering the title, "the Bride" except you meet the final requirement, you may end up not being called wife, which means you miss out on the marriage ceremony, the wedding doors may be closed against you.

Also, from the scriptures we read last, we can see that the finest of the pure white linen purchased for her to wear, represents good deeds of God's holy people. It means that even if beauty and physical features draw a man to a lady for a relationship, it will still take her inner beauty (good character) to secure a marriage.

"But I have this complaint against you. You don't love me or each other as you did at first! Look how far you have fallen! Turn back to me and do the works you did at first. If you don't repent, I will come and remove your lamp stand from its place among the churches." Revelations 2:5

The just shall live by faith (revelational) as the scripture says it, but the just shall be preserved by the deeds of his faith (the works produced). However, retaining our status as a bride of Jesus can only be guaranteed if our works are equally right with our confession. Anything outside of this means that your place among the saints will be substituted. Though you took part in the wedding process as a bride, but you will not partake in the marriage proper. "You don't love me..." (Rev 2:4) Jesus needs more love from you today! It is a big concern!

THE AFFECTION BETWEEN JESUS AND HIS BRIDE (THE CHURCH)

A friend of mine, Wale Odeniyi, defines love as "true affection from a sincere heart." I love this definition. Personally, I see love as an overwhelming affection that propels a man to give everything without considering the consequences or the pains involved.

Also, there are four things that I have discovered that can never be hidden, no matter how you try to pretend or cover up. These are: ignorance, knowledge, cough and Love. They freely express themselves. "There are three things that amaze me- no, four things that I don't understand; how an eagle glides through the sky, how a snake slithers on a rock, how a ship navigates the ocean, how a man loves a woman" (Proverbs. 30:18-19).

God has an established order: every soul that sins shall die. He also knows that the only unbeatable platform that could handle this exchange of life for death is a deeper level of love. As He designed it at creation, the highest dimension of love a human being can express is the type between him and his wife. Love is one of the greatest dimensions of the Father and Son relationship, which they expressed towards humanity. "God loved the world so much that He gave His one and only Son, so that everyone who believes in him will not perish but have eternal life" (John 3:16). It is glaring that the bridegroom has never failed on his part of showing and expressing his love towards humanity, but unrequited love is a terrible thing to do.

ONE- SIDED AFFECTION

Love is one thing that cannot be hidden, no matter how hard you try at pretending. Some people see love as an abstract concept, but the truth of the matter is that it can speak.

Love is the true nature of God the Father that Jesus has replicated. The nature of God deposited in man was lost after man fell in the Garden of Eden. This is the reason why today men have opted for lust instead of pure and sacrificial love. There is a yoking, which occurs in a true sexual relationship. The best way God could express His love for humanity again was to open up the relationship channel, one that will deepen the attachment to one another. The love between a husband and wife is a mysterious feeling that goes beyond human explanation.

If you have ever been in love, I mean true love; you will discover that the beauty of every marriage is not in the amount of material acquisitions, but the mutual love that flows between the husband and wife. The frustration there also lies in a divided attention or shared love. An expression of love is demonstrated by the ability to lay down one's life for another. When a man tells a woman that he loves her; my next question is, "Are you saying that you can lay down your life for her?" Can you exchange your life by taking her place in death? If the answer is no or uncertain, then you don't know what you are talking about. True love is unconditional and it doesn't die. But today, the body of Christ is bedeviled by the spirit of division and divorce, which is not a constituent of our heavenly DNA; it's not in our Father's genes.

Little wonder, Jesus demonstrates this true love to His bride, the Church. "For God loved the world so much that he gave his one and only son (Jesus), so that who believes in him will not perish but have eternal life." (John 3:16). "But God showed his great love for us by sending Christ to die for us while we were still sinners" (Romans 5:8).

Integrity is part of God's core values; He will never demand from a man what He himself can't give. He first demonstrated this love towards us as it is explicated in the relationship between the bridegroom, Jesus, and His bride, the church. However, the snag in this relationship is that it has been a one-sided affair. The church has had dual commitments, i.e. cheating on her spouse. This is one of the sources of God's heartache.

Jesus cried out, "If you love me, obey my commandments" (John 14:15). "Jesus replied, "The most important commandment is this. Listen, O Israel! (The church) the Lord our God is the one and only Lord. And you must love the Lord your God with all your heart, all your soul, all your mind and all your strength." (Mark 12:29-30). He is asking for our singular and total commitment to Him.

Jesus is saying to the Church," If truly you love me, you will not break the rules of our engagement." We can see clearly from the above scriptures that Jesus loves the church dearly but His love is unrequited. Though the church still claims to be the bride, she is ridden with a hidden agenda, selfish interest, divided attention and loyalty, and lack of adequate preparation for the real marriage in eternity. This is the state of the church which still waves her insincere hands to Jesus during meetings as a sign of total surrender, whereas her lifestyle is contrary to what she professes.

DECEPTIVE HEART OF THE BRIDE

One of the most delicate and vital organs of man is the heart. The state of a man's heart determines the course of his life. A man's attitude and altitude in life is a function of what he has stored in his heart over time. A committed or a divided loyalty is a function of the state of the heart. A divided heart would produce divided attention, allegiance, affection, etc. God created a man with the ability and power to make choices. This is one of the features that separate man from angels. Angels are mechanical in operation, i.e. they have no self-willing, however, man was designed to make decisions, created with the ability to think, imagine and act based on his decisions. The heart is the seat of this process. "And you must love the Lord your God with all your heart, all your soul, all your mind and all your strength." (Mark 12:30).

By inference, it is very possible for a person to love with a partial heart. This also shows that not every confessed love is sincere and genuine and heartfelt. The heart and focus of the Church of Jesus Christ have been shifted and diverted to pursuing other lovers. When a man's love for Jesus waxes cold, you will notice it in different manifestations, such as idolatry, self-centredness, love of money, lies, covenant breaking lawlessness, deception, unfaithfulness, greed, manipulation, hatred, etc.

The truth of the matter is that as far as Jesus is concerned, there is no place for a partial and lukewarm lover. It is either your love is hot for Him or it is cold. This was the charge Jesus laid against the church of Ephesus and it's still the same spirit operating in today's church. "But I have this complaint against you. You don't love me or each other as you did at first." (Revelations 2:4)

Friends, you don't need to be told that Jesus is not happy with His bride, and our love is the only thing that confirms our position in His life. There is a profession of dead love towards Him and our brethren. It is disheartening that among the ekklesia today, you will find a great deal of hatred, malice, deception, greed, self-centredness, a gathering of deceivers instead of believers and a brood of greedy men. The church has become a place where there is no provision and room for the widows, orphans, fatherless, poor and the rest of the less privileged. It has also become a gathering that only honors the rich and relegates the poor; where sentiments, tribalism, nepotism, sexism and special treatment are the order of the day. You can't expect this kind of church to truly love her bridegroom the way she ought to.

Men of right hearts are very few in the church of Jesus Christ today. No wonder the scriptures warns: "Guard your heart above all else, for it determines the course of your life" (Proverbs 4:23). Therefore, what you make out of your life is a function of your heart, so guard it jealously. This was the prayer of David, a revelational discovery in Psalm 51:10: "Create in me a clean heart, O God. Renew a loyal spirit within me." No wonder God refers to David as man after this own heart. I wish this should become our prayer point from today; a request for a clean heart and renewed loyal spirit towards our bridegroom, Jesus. This is so that at every point in time nothing will be strong enough to share our precious hearts with the Lord.

CHURCH: THE PROMISCUOUS LOVER

There was a man who really loved his wife by every standard of measurement to the extent that this intoxicating love was visible to everyone. In fact, every other woman craved for this kind of love from her husband. Among other things, she was a signatory to all her husband's bank accounts and majority of the assets were in her name. However, the irony of this scenario was that her husband never enjoyed any moment with his wife. This woman rather preferred making other men outside happy by giving them attention rather than the man that was spending his life living for her.

Friends, this scenario is just an exact type of the relationship between Jesus and the Church. With everything Jesus has done for us and is still doing on a daily basis, we have lost the true heart of commitment. Our body is in the relationship, but our heart is far from it. We have forgotten that true relationship is an offspring of pure affection from a sincere heart.

A promiscuous lover is one who has many sexual partners. A promiscuous lifestyle is typified by an unstable, unpredictable, and inconsistent life. This is somewhat true about our church today. The church today has come to the highest level of religious practices instead of cultivating a true relationship. Pastors and other ministry heads are wooing, lobbying, seducing and manipulating people into their local churches. Correspondingly, there is an increase in attendance and membership. However, the number of men and women that are truly committed to God is getting fewer every day. They are baptizing these people into their own personal ambition, using the church or ministry as a ruse to perpetrate evil. They are not ready to introduce them to the true lover of the church, Jesus Christ.

It is very painful that the Church Jesus Christ died for has now deviated from the truth, going after other gods in idolatry such as gold; i.e. money and material things, goals, i.e. their personal ambition, all in the name of Church of God PLC or Incorporated. What about the mad rush for fame and competitive spirit, deception and the publicity of personal agenda, the goddess which is the spirit of adultery and idolatry? Other banes of today's church include divorce, extra-marital affairs, sexual perversion, self-worship, praise and manipulation.

This was actually the revelation of the prophet Isaiah in Chapter 4 of the book of Isaiah, about today's church, which many have misinterpreted. "In that day so few men will be left that seven women will fight for each man, saying, "Let us all marry you! We will provide our own food and clothing only let us take your name so we don't be mocked as old maids." (Isaiah 4:1). The last part in King James Version says, "Only let us be called by thy name, to take away our reproach." The first time I heard this scripture was through a young lady who felt that the population of women outnumbered those of men. She believed that if a woman could find a very committed man for a relationship, she would be grateful by reason of the scripture quoted above. It took years for the Holy Spirit to reveal that it wasn't the mind of God and the true interpretation of that scripture. Meanwhile, many men have taken advantage of this scripture to marry many wives while some are engaged in multiple dating; going out with more than one woman at the same time while some sisters had put themselves in a disadvantaged position to be helped or pitied.

The true prophetic interpretation of the scripture is thus: the women are referring to the Body of Christ, which is the bride or the church, while the man is the source of covering, the solution provider, the protection, the glory and the object of reverence.

In this prophetic scenario, the seven women are a type of the Church Jesus spoke about through John in the book of Revelation 2 and 3, the churches of Ephesus, Smyrna, Pergamum, Thyatira, Sardis, Philadelphia and Laodicea. Each of these churches could not perfectly meet the designed standard of Jesus. They all came to Him with their individual agenda like the women in Isaiah chapter four; they are not seeking true love or sincere affection, but are on a mission that their own reproach may be taken away.

The truth is: it is only you who know why you have come to the Master. For some, membership is used to get a godly spouse, some are there to make the right business connections, some like the branding of the assembly, and others because they like the pastor without knowing the God of the pastor. Some want to make new associates and acquaintances. How many of us have come to worship and serve God for who He is, rather than what we can get from Him. The heart of Jesus is still bleeding for this unproductive union between Himself and the Church.

Until the Church comes into a place of sincerity and truth in our relationship with Jesus, where we shall choose to have only one lover, i.e. Jesus, our efforts in the self- defined relationship will not have eternal values and everything shall be equivalent to dead works.

STANDARD FOR THE TRUE BRIDE

It is a statement of fact that not all women are wife materials. If a man will not settle for anything less, just because of the token bride price he is paying where it is applicable, how much more Jesus who paid an unprecedented price for the Church, an unquantifiable price to purchase this bride? We shouldn't be expecting someone in the class of Jesus to settle for a bride with spot and wrinkles, considering the weight of His investment. Jesus also likened this standard to the preparation of would- be brides waiting for the arrival of the bridegroom.

The Kingdom of Heaven can be illustrated by the story of the ten bridesmaids (virgins) who took their lamps and went to meet the bridegroom. Five of them were foolish, and five were wise. The five who were foolish didn't take enough oil for their lamps, but the other five were wise enough to take along extra oil.

When the bridegroom was delayed, they all became drowsy and fell asleep. At midnight they were roused by the shout, 'Look, the bridegroom is coming! Come out and meet him! All the bridesmaids got up and prepared their lamps. Then the five foolish one asked the others, please give us some of your oil because our lamps are going out; But the others replied we don't have enough for all of us. Go to a shop and buy some for yourselves. But while they were gone to buy oil, the bridegroom came. Then those who were ready went in with Him to the marriage feast, and the door was locked. When the other five bridesmaids returned, they stood outside, calling, 'Lord! Open the door for us! But he called back, 'Believe me, I don't know you! So you too, must keep watch! For you don't know the day or the hour of my return. Matthew 25:1-13

PRINCIPLES TO BE NOTED IN THESE SCRIPTURES

Everything in the Kingdom centers on relationship, not religion. Jesus often loved to use the relationship between two sincere lovers to drive home His point.

Five of them were foolish. (Matthew 25:2).

Jesus shows us that it's not enough to be emotionally attached; there is the place of wisdom and revelation in the relationship, which He is demanding from us. (Matthew 25:2). This also suggests that it's not enough to come to Jesus at the altar call, there are expectations. Growth is expected from our relationship with Jesus, and not stagnation on the altar of religion.

They didn't take enough oil for their lamps. (Matthew 25:3).

The religious church, without an understanding of how the true relationship works, doesn't have what it takes to survive and meet the daily needs of her lover, Jesus. Inevitably the lives of the members would lack grace, divine enablement and resources for the next level. They built a monument instead of setting their hearts on movement.

But the other five were wise enough to take enough oil. (Matthew 25:4).

We need to strive to be wise. The wise ones represent those who follow Jesus by revelation, who have an eternal purpose and imbibe values such as the devotion to the word of God, prayer and fellowship. These are men and women who have gone beyond the outer courts where the crowds are milling around in the inner sanctuary of the most Holy Place; where they can see God for themselves. There will always be a breaking point when the natural strength of man will fail, but whatever grace you have stored up over the years for yourself in the place of a deep relationship will determine how far you will go.

They were all drowsy while the bridegroom delayed. (Matthew 25:5).

It doesn't matter how long it takes, the promise of the glorious day will surely come, where the prepared bride, i.e. the church, shall meet her love, Jesus, and they both shall be forever and ever. Expectation is the mother of manifestation. The prepared church shall never be disappointed no matter how long it may tarry.

The foolish five begged others to give them some oil, because their lamps were going out. (Matthew 25:8);

You will know the activities of the foolish brides, i.e. the religious church, by their traditional ways of doing things; relying on second hand revelation which they received through another medium. They are not ready to seek for themselves that which would be able to sustain them in the time of challenges, but rather indolently seek support from others who have paid the price. It also means that anyone who does not have constant and continuous relationship with the bridegroom, Jesus, will soon expire or become obsolete with respect to the move of God.

We should also learn that even in the midst of corporate anointing, there is a need for every individual to be anointed by the Holy Spirit for the task assigned to each of us. Each of us has got to come to a place of individual interaction and fellowship with the bridegroom. This goes beyond the corporate worship.

But while the prepared bridesmaids went in with the bridegroom to the feast, the foolish ones went for the oil. (Matthew 25:9-10.)

The Church of Jesus must be accurate in knowing the timing, the season and also discerning the moves of God on earth per time. This also reveals that the Church is not only called to do the right things, but to do the things right at the right time.

When the foolish virgins returned, they stood outside, calling Lord, Lord! Open the door for us. (Matthew 25:11). Emotional worship is a product of carnality. The Church can't satisfy and meet the needs of the bridegroom using human emotions, rather it is by the Spirit

The doors were locked. (Matthew 25:11b).

It does not matter how good your starting point might be, without growth, increase and fruitfulness, you are a failure as far as heaven is concerned. It also signifies that the end point is just as important and maybe much more important to the bridegroom as your beginning. They all started on the same track, however, they forgot that one thing was needful.

I knew you not (Matthew 25:12).

Jesus does not keep records of pretentious religious activities. The church is using head knowledge to establish God's truth. However, only a meaningful, revelational relationship with the bridegroom can build a structure that would stand the test of time.

You might have been building for years and yet don't have any records in heaven. Beloved, let us examine ourselves.

Therefore, it is not enough to be part of the Church of Jesus, individual commitment and relationship must be measured. And don't forget, you won't be rewarded for operating based on the way you feel, there is an established order that can never be changed.

How prepared are you for the marriage feast of the Lamb? Are you qualified? Do you fit the bill? Do self-examination today and be sincere enough to yourself. Then you can turn a new leaf, not minding what it will cost you just to meet the bridegroom's standard and specification.

This is the only safeguard for all your labor and activities for the kingdom, or else they will all amount to nothing. Ask yourself as a minister of the gospel, how many members of my large congregation will be acceptable on that day? Preparation determines performance. The bridegroom will definitely come back for His bride, will you be counted worthy?

Chapter Five

The Church: The Temple of God

"I will prefer getting to heaven to find written on my account: "... he lived all his life pleasing God" than to have"... though he built the biggest structure for God on earth"

"And what union can there be between God's temple and Idols? For we are the temple of the living God. As God said; I will live in them and walk among them, I will be their God, and they will be my people"

2 Corinthians 6:16

The temple is a common word among the religious circles. It is not a Christian thing; it is a universal term that cuts across many religions.

A temple can be described as "a building used for the worship of spiritual beings and deities." The Jews had temples for the worship of Jehovah. There were also the temple of Diana, a Greek goddess at Ephesus (See Acts 19:27, 28, 34, 35), the temple of Dagon, a Philistine god (See I Chronicles 10:10) and Isaiah 5:5), the Hindus and Buddhists temples and the temple of Confucius. These underscore the fact that temples are places of spiritual habitation.

However, for Christians, the temple refers to us as the house of God or a center of worship. "But as for me, I will come into thy house in the multitude of thy fear will I worship toward thy Holy temple" (Psalm 5:7 KJV). "But the Lord is in his holy Temple; the Lord still rules from heaven. He watches everyone closely, examining every person on earth. (Psalm 11:4) "I bow before your Holy Temple as I worship. I praise your name for your unfailing love and faithfulness: for your promises are backed by all the honor of your name" (Psalm 138:2). Therefore, the Temple can be viewed as the house of the Lord, and not necessarily a physical structure or building.

GOD'S CONCEPT ABOUT TEMPLE

The word, "concept" can be taken for an idea, design and philosophy behind something. Here we are looking at God's own idea of the word, temple. In driving at a meaningful point, there is need to compare the Old and New Testament Scriptures to discover what the Temple represented in each dispensation.

God, the Creator of heaven and earth, always has a design and concept in mind before creating anything. Therefore, if we will live meaningful and fulfilling lives, they can only be achieved by doing things according to His own concept and design.

Originally, God created man with the ability or capacity for relationship and worship. That's why it was easy for man to understand the sound of God, even after sinning in the Garden of Eden. (See Genesis 3:8). Before that time, Adam and Eve did not have a particular location for worship, because the entire Garden of Eden was God's realm and filled with His glory which was conducive for worship. But since man was sent packing from the Garden, that presence became transient and fleeting, and could not be domiciled.

Therefore, one major place where God meets with His people and where the people came to worship and plead for their sins in the Old Testament was the Temple, since the ability to relate and hear from God had been destroyed. "But the lord is in His Holy Temple, the Lord still rules from heaven. He watches everyone closely, examining every person on earth" (Psalm 11:4). This scripture indicates that God wasn't permanently living in the Temple, but when the right offerings and sacrifices were made and accepted, the presence of God came down.

Even at that, the temple was considered to be a consecrated, sacred building for the Lord. In terms of the biblical usage of the word "temple", two prominent words in the original Greek interpretation are "naio," which describes it as a shrine and also "hieron" meaning a sacred place or denotes the entire sanctuary itself e.g. the Temple at Jerusalem. If the two Greek words present the idea of the temple as a shrine, a place of worship and sacred, that is a consecrated place, we can take a position that the real concept in the mind of God was that He was creating a platform where He could still relate with man despite his fallen state, though at a cost.

TEMPLE IN DISPENSATION

There have been diverse dispensations that have come and gone. These dispensations or periods were actually designed by God for His own purpose and fulfillment of prophesies. Each of them has been characterized by various activities, which were originally ordered by God as part of His program and tools to usher mankind to the perfect state that He had designed him for.

Therefore, the operations and the clear shift in the move of the Spirit which manifests on earth summarizes the dispensations into two main parts. First, the activities from creation to the birth of Jesus as the Old Testament, where God related with men through prophets and priests starting from the fall of Adam and Eve. Second, the New Testament era which summarizes the events from the birth of Jesus till this very day. We are part of this dispensation, where God relates with man one on one through the Holy Spirit by the reason of the sacrifice of the precious blood of Jesus .

Another name for dispensation, apart from the order and testament, is a covenant, which we can see in Galatians 4: 21-26: "Tell me, you who want to live under the law; do you know what the law actually says? The Scriptures say that Abraham had two sons, one from his slave with one from his freeborn wife. The son of the slave wife was born in a human attempt to bring about the fulfillment of God's promise, but the son of the freeborn wife was born as God's own fulfillment of his promise. These two women serve as an illustration of God's two covenants. The first woman, Hagar, represents Mount Sinai, where people received the law that enslaved them. And now Jerusalem is just like Mount Sinai in Arabia, because she and her children live in slavery to the law. But the other woman, Sarah, represents the heavenly Jerusalem; she is the free woman and she is our mother" (Galatians 4:21-26). (See also Gen 16: 15)

From the two dispensations or covenants above, one describes the season when men were struggling by, his power or human calculations to reach and to please God; adopting a fleshly approach to fulfilling the will of God. Let's imagine the kind of worship Abraham was bringing to God at this dispensation, though he loved God, feared Him and always wanted to do His will, but it was a product of his human effort. However, the second covenant stands out because it is the place where Abraham aligned himself to the will of God and in due season. God brought to pass His promises that no flesh would glory in. There was no place for the flesh or human efforts as this kind of worship was void of human's calculations.

THE TEMPLE AND THE OLD COVENANT

We have established the fact that the temple has a universal acceptance by religious people. Another word that has a semblance of it is the Tabernacle. The Oxford Advanced Learners Dictionary defines Tabernacle as "a place of worship for some group of Christians or a small place of worship that could be moved, used by the Jews in ancient times when they were travelling in the desert." This word is used interchangeably with temple in Scriptures.

In trying to paint the picture of God's expectation of his Church as His own temple we would need to look at parallels of the temple in the old covenant. We would also look at the way worship as then, with a view to discerning the mind of God for this new dispensation. This would help the church get to the point of accuracy in worship rather than trying to please God by flesh, i.e. human activities.

That first covenant between God and Israel (a type of the Church) had regulations for worship and a place of worship here on earth. There were two rooms in that Tabernacle (tent). In the first room were a lamp stand, a table, and sacred loaves of bread on the table. This room was called the holy place. Then there was a curtain, and it was the second room called the Most Holy Place. In that room was an incense altar and a wooden chest called the Ark of the Covenant, which was covered with gold on all sides. Inside the ark was a gold jar containing manna and tablets of the covenant. Above the Ark were the Cherubim of divine glory, whose wings stretched out over the Ark's cover, the place of atonement. We cannot explain these things in detail now. When they were all in place, the priests regularly entered the first room as they performed their religious duties. But only the high priest ever entered the most Holy Place, and only once a year. And he always offered blood for his own sins and for the sins of the people. The entrance to the Most Holy Place was not freely open as long as the Tabernacle and the system it represented were still in use. This is an illustration pointing to the present time. For the gifts and sacrifices, that the priests offer are not able to cleanse the consciences of the people who bring them. For that old system deals only with food and drink and various cleansing ceremonies- physical regulations that were in effect until a better system could be established. (Hebrews 9: 1-10).

Beloved, let's not lose sight of the fact that our emphasis is to see what exactly the church, i.e. you and I as the temple of God in the new dispensation should represent. Therefore, it is necessary to examine the pattern of this Temple in the Old Covenant and its representations. This is the essence of the Scriptures above.

THE DEFICIENCY OF OLD COVENANT TEMPLE

Every new technology brings a better and improved way of doing things and renders the Old order obsolete. This is why the old temple was relegated to the dustbins of history; it could not carry any weight in the spirit any longer. It doesn't matter who is still operating with this old system as far as God is concerned, there has been a shift in the spirit. You can't operate in the new move of God with an old mindset. Hebrews 8:7 affirms: "If the first covenant had been faultless, there would have been no need for a second covenant to replace it. But when God found fault with the people, he said, The day is coming, says the Lord, when I will make a new covenant with the people of Israel and Judah (Israel typifies the Church, while Judah represents praise or worship)."

Some of the deficiencies noticed in the old temple include the following:

The old order was stagnant instead of moving. Therefore, it didn't have the capacity to fit into the next move of God. Whose agenda was forcefully advancing on a timely basis. Therefore, anything that would impede that progression must be done away with.

The old system of worship had a religious experience that had the power to draw people closer to the presence of God without bringing enough energy to take them into the very presence of God. All they had was a sampling experience and not the real deal. Only the priest and High priest could gain access into the presence of God as represented by the holy and Most Holy Place. Also, the old covenant placed a premium on human efforts. It depended on the efforts of the high priest who must offer sacrifices for himself and the congregation. Also, the people brought animals for the various sacrifices and offerings in the temple.

Classification, segregation, stratification and superiority existed within the operating system of this "old technology". Not every member of the congregation could have access to God by himself or herself except the selected and privileged few, i.e. the Levites and the priests, whereas God is demanding and craving for a relationship with every individual. Today, this system is still being enjoyed by some ministers who lord it over the flock of Jesus, instead of teaching them how each individual can have a good relationship with the King. These men are enjoying the benefits of being the middlemen. Hear this: God will wipe them all away sooner than you think, so that He can take His place in the life of his people. The old order was such that the worship of God was not an everyday affair. Even the high priest went in once a year. This created certain impediments and logjam in the spirit. However, God has called us to liberty in worship in the timing and location.

It was a process of worship that moved by external and physical obligations instead of internal consideration, i.e. the state of the heart, which produces eternal values. The same error is still operational in many churches today; decision making with very carnal minds, doing everything with human wisdom and educational information and spending so much on physical structures and branding. However, they spend little or no time on those things that have eternal values, i.e. the people. There is nothing wrong in acquiring a standard and conducive worship center; nevertheless, it shouldn't be a strategy for drawing men together. This is not the essence of living; God doesn't live in a building or structures made by men's hands. "David found favor with God and asked for the privilege of building a permanent Temple for the God of Jacob. But it was Solomon who actually built it. However, the Most High doesn't live in Temples made by human hands. As the Scripture says: "Heaven is my throne, and the earth is my footstool. Could you build me a temple as good as that? Ask the Lord. Could you build me such a resting place? Didn't my hands make both heavens and earth?" (Acts 7: 46-50). Prophet Isaiah also confirms this position in Isaiah: 66:1-7. Apostle Paul reaffirms this claim in speaking to the men of Athens, a religious group of people and idol worshipers in Acts 17:24: "He is the God who made heaven and earth, He doesn't live in man-made temples."

THE PATTERN OF THE NEW DISPENSATION TEMPLE

The temple of the old order is a pointer to what the temple fully represents in the new dispensation. "We are carefully joined together in him, becoming a holy temple for the Lord. Through him you gentiles are also being made part of this dwelling where God lives by his Spirit" (Eph 2:21-22).

Since the new move of God redefines the temple as human based, the dwelling place of God, this implies that even in the Old Testament, every building couldn't be a temple. Temples were consciously built with dimensions, prescription, and precision. In the New Testament, our lives must have dimensions, which are about the length, breadth and width of our temple, i.e. our capacity and the space we give to God in our lives.

Let's take a cue from the Temple of Solomon. (I King 6: 1-2, 6, 7, 11-13).

(1) It was in midspring, in the Month of Zif (which means second month), during the fourth year of Solomon's reign that he began to construct the Temple of the Lord. This was 480 years after the people of Israel were rescued from their slavery in the land of Egypt. (2) The Temple was 90 feet long, 30 feet wide, and 45 feet high (in Hebrew 60 cubits, i.e. 27.6 meters long, 20 cubits, i.e. 9.2 meters wide, and 30 cubits, i.e. 13.8 meters high. (3) The complex was three stories high, the bottom floor 71/2 feet wide, the second floor 9feet wide, and the top floor 101/2 feet wide. The rooms were connected to the walls of the temple by beams resting on ledges built out from the walls. So the beams were not inserted into the walls themselves. (4) The stones used in the construction of the temple were finished at the quarry, so there was no sound of hammer, ax or any other iron tool at the building site. (5). Then the Lord gave this message to Solomon: Concerning this temple you are building, if you keep all my decrees and regulations and obey

all my commands, I will fulfill through you all the promise I made to your father, David. 13. I will live among the Israelites and will never abandon them.

THE PRINCIPLES BEHIND THE NEW TEMPLE BUILDING

The Old Testament was a shadow or type of the real things God was planning to come into the New Covenant. We shall critically look at the mind of God concerning the new order by cross-checking the content of the old.

From the first verse, in yielding ourselves unto God as a building, it must be a deliberate, conscious, planned, purposeful and willing action. Sure, there are other activities craving for our attention. However, there is a set time for every form of building in the plans of God. You must work with divine timing.

In verse 2, the temple which Solomon built for the Lord, was 90 feet long, 30 feet wide and 45 feet high. The implication of this is that God cannot fill us beyond the space we give unto Him. The figures, 90, 30 and 45feet are very significant and prophetic. The human being is a spirit, living in a body, having a soul, i.e. he operates in three realms. If 90 is divided into 3 places we would have 30 in each place. A 90 per cent grading is excellent, but not yet perfect. There is still a 10 percent left, meaning that it can still be better. Dividing 90 by 2 gives us 45. God originally made man with the ability to access heaven while ruling the earth. This was the dimension Solomon operated in which was the highest of the Old Testament records. The best of men that made things happen supernaturally in the Scriptures operated between 60 and 90 per cent capacity and ability of God. This reveals that the few men whose walk with God was not fully perfect, but was very close to God's standard, such men like Moses, Abraham, Isaac, Jacob, Elijah, David, Samson, etc. had their points of encounter with God where God walked with them. The 90 percent of divinity in these men made them look like God on earth, while the remaining 10 percent gave them the ability to relate with their world. But for Enoch, the Bible record that he walked with God for a long time that the human nature in him was non-existent. He couldn't relate with the world system so God had to take him away. "When Enoch was 65 years old, he became the father of Methuselah. After the birth of Methuselah, Enoch lived in close fellowship with God for another 300 years and he had other sons and daughters. He lived 365 years walking in close fellowship with God. Then one day he disappeared, because God took him (Genesis 5: 21-23). So he did not know death. This was also the testimony of Elijah. This is the level God is calling us into as New Testament believers.

Jesus explained it further by using the parable of the farmer scattering seeds on different grounds and their yields. With respect to the fertile soil: "still other seeds fell on fertile soil and they produced a crop that was thirty (30), sixty (60) and even a hundred (100) times as much as had been planted. Anyone with ears to hear should listen and understand" (Matthew13: 8-9).

The significance of this is that the 90 per cent of the Old Testament cannot work in this new scheme of God. The 10 per cent remaining is of great value as Jesus is coming back for a church without spots and wrinkles. He did this to present her (Church) to Himself as a glorious church without a spot and wrinkle or any other blemish. Instead, she will be holy and without fault (Ephesians 5:27). "And the Church is his body; it is made full and complete by Christ, who fills all things everywhere with himself" (Ephesians 1:23). Jesus is interested in filling up every space In our lives, not thirty or sixty or even ninety per cent, he wants total control. This is the only way we can exercise complete dominion and become "gods" on earth. Today, a lot of us in the body of Christ are measuring the space, which He can occupy in our lives thereby limiting the move of God. Some others lives have been occupied by greed, mammon, and hypocrisy. How do we ask unbelievers to give their lives to Jesus when we are yet to surrender ours totally to the Master?

We would see from I Kings 6:6 that this edifice was made up of three-floor building with every room connected to the wall of the Temple. It is very important that everything in our lives must be connected to the source of life. As the three-storey building was connected to the Temple, which represents the place of worship, so every part of our lives, spirit, soul and body must not only submit to God, but must bring glory to Him. In verse 7, the stones used in the construction of the Temple were finished from the quarry so there was no single sound of hammer or any tool at the site. The stone here represents the revelation of God, which cannot be received by your own working. It is a finished business so it is not the product of your efforts or technology. It is by the Spirit. Therefore, we can only survive by revelation, not by struggle, tradition or human ideology or philosophies.

In verses 11 and 12, God gave instructions concerning how the Temple would be built. It is not enough to have zeal for God, His requirements and specifications must be followed to the letter if He is going to occupy your life and make use of you. Obedience is the only way to show that we believe His revelation.

Verse 13 says, God indicated His intention to abide permanently if the structures are built according to the heavenly template. God wants to abide in us, but are we ready to abide in Him? Today, there are a lot of temples, but how many of them are carriers of His presence or carcasses of the devil? Is God in your temple or is the devil occupying the throne of your life? I pray that your labor for the kingdom will not be in vain. There is no vacuum in nature as well as in the spirit; something must drive you. Are you ready to allow God to take up permanent residence in your life?

THE OFFICE OF THE PRIEST IN THE TEMPLE

When we talk about the office of the priest in the Temple, we are not searching for one of the rooms where the priest used to stay to work, but we are referring to the responsibility of the priest within the Temple in the Old Testament. There were some basic services or rituals, which could only be performed by the priests. It is therefore expedient to define who a priest is and his specific functions in the service of God in the temple.

"Assign the Levites to Aaron and his sons. They have been given from among all the people of Israel to serve as their assistants. Appoint Aaron and his sons to carry out the duties of the priesthood. But any unauthorized person who goes too near the sanctuary must be put to death" Numbers 3:9-10

"When these things were all in place, the priests regularly entered the first room as they performed their religious duties. But only the high priest ever entered the most Holy Place, and only once in a year. And always offered blood for his own sins and for the sins the people had committed in ignorance" Hebrews 9:6-7

"As was the custom of the priests, he was chosen by lot to enter the sanctuary of the Lord and burn incense" Luke 1:9

These Scriptures help us to clarify the core functions of every called priest. Firstly, priesthood is not a political appointment that a man admires and pursues with human energy. It is God who does the calling. (See Numbers 3:10).

Secondly, a priest is involved with the offering of different sacrifices and worship unto God.

In terms of the sacrifices, the High Priest entered the most Holy Place once in a year to offer blood for the sins of himself and the people, so that their worship could be accepted. But today, Jesus personally handles this great task through his once-and-for-all death on the cross for humanity, thus abolishing the annual ritual.

"In fact, according to the law of Moses, nearly everything was purified with blood. For without the shedding of blood, there is no forgiveness" Hebrews 9:22

The true definition of ministry is in the offering of our service to God and humanity from a pure and undefiled heart. Every true ministry should be life- giving. This is not a service that comes from the soulish realm of man, like humanitarian services, voluntary and non-government organization services, but true service that is borne out of the spirit. This kind of service can only come from a temple where Jesus resides, or else it will be described as self-gratification, carnality and eye-service.

"Examine yourselves to see if your faith is genuine. Test yourselves. Surely you know that Jesus Christ is among you" 2 Corinthians 13:5

Examine yourselves; whether ye be in faith, prove your own selves. Know ye not your own selves, how that Jesus Christ is in you, except ye be reprobates (KJV).

The services that will have eternal value are those which emanate from the Spirit. Our lives, the temples of the Lord, where Jesus should reside, have now become abodes for greed, malice, hatred and every work of the flesh. Let us examine ourselves, what kind of services are we giving?

The third paramount duty of every priest in the Temple is Worship. This is the essence of our living and the greatest demand of God from us. "I bow before your holy Temple as I worship. I praise your name for your unfailing love and faithfulness; (Psalm 138:20). "Everything on earth will worship you; they will sing your praises, shouting your name in glorious songs" (Psalm 66:4).

Did we notice that the last scripture above does not say "every human being will worship you", rather it says "everything on earth", meaning every creature (both living and nonliving) which means that every cry of the birds in the air is a praise unto the Creator. The fishes in the seas and wild animals in the forests, as long as they are manifesting their intrinsic character traits, they are fulfilling a purpose and thereby bringing glory, honor and worship to God.

Wait a minute! What about you, who was created in God's image and patterned after His likeness? Please, note that if your lifestyle does not bring worship to God, it is actually bringing glory to the devil. You are created to worship God; who or what receives your worship must be one who is worthy to. I pray that every aspect of your life will bring worship unto the Lord.

Moreover, it is not every worship that comes to God, your worship must be purified; it must be from a sincere or genuine altar. God sees your heart and checks your inner motives. In the Old Testament, priests were selected on the basis of the Levitical order, i.e. they had to be descendants of Aaron; and they were the only people who could present the corporate worship of the church in the wilderness to the Lord. However, today it is not the function of any pastor, or any minister to bring the worship of others; everyone must present their worship to God with the pastor as a guide not an intermediary. Yes! Jesus has pulled down the wall of partitions and boundaries between God and us; therefore we all have personal access to God. What a delightsome experience.

"But you are not like that, for you are a chosen people. You are royal priests, a holy nation, God's own possession. As a result, you can show others the goodness of God, for He called you out of the darkness into his wonderful light" 1 Peter 2:9

"And you have caused them to become a Kingdom of priests for our God. And they will reign on the earth" Revelations 5:10

Everyone that has been washed by the blood of Jesus is a temple and carrier of God's power and can also serve in the office of a priest; those who have the ability and grace to bring worship to God on earth.

The church as God's temple is where Christ dwells. It is not a matter of physical structure, as God cannot be tied down to any building or a location. As carriers of his glory, it is our presence that makes a sanctuary sacred. Therefore, our worship should go to God at all times and from everything we do because the flesh can never bring worship to God. Also, our worship must not be mechanical, methodical and calculative; rather it must be by the Spirit.

"But the time is coming, indeed, it's here now when the true worshipers will worship the father in spirit and in truth. The father is looking for those who will worship him that way. For God is Spirit, so those who worship him must worship in spirit and truth" (John 4:23-24).

The implication of this scripture is firstly; not every worshipper is a true worshipper of God, even though they confess Him. Secondly, the Father needs true worship to survive in the midst of the falsehood and deceptive worship that flow everywhere. These are mere pollutions designed by the devil to make man a perpetual religious person. The Father is searching for genuine worshippers. Thirdly, the word "true" or "truth" connotes the identity of Jesus Christ and implies that without accepting Jesus and having a relationship with Him, your worship can never come to the Father because He is the Truth.

"Jesus said to the people who believed in him, you are truly my disciples, if you remain faithful to my teachings. And you will know the truth and the truth will set you free" (John 8:31-32)

"Jesus told him, "I am the way, the truth, and the life. No one can come to the father except through me (John 14:6).

Since every believer is a temple of God. It follows therefore, that our local church should be a gathering of temples, where God is resident. Many ministries today are very proud of their large congregations while some others are still striving to grow big. Only very few examine and care to know the state of their flock: are they really temples of God, real carriers of God's presence? Don't forget that these temples can never be empty, if they don't contain God, they will contain something else. This is why churches that are fixing global problems have become a headache to God. Friends, pause for a minute and ask, am I a temple of the Lord? Be sincere to yourself and do something about your answer today.

The wrong emphasis on the structural building as the church needs to be deleted from our minds. The denominational competitive spirit in the church as to who owns the best architectural designs within our region is nothing but a demonic spirit that is put in place by the enemy to distract the Church.

I once heard a minister preach that one of the things that make a great ministry is the size of the acquired properties and the structures erected. The question now is, "must we buy an estate before we can fellowship together?" What God demands from us is our fellowship and His concern and emphasis is on the people, not the structure.

Today, the church, which is supposed to feed the poor, is tasking the poor to contribute out of nothing for the building project. They do this by frustrating the less privileged and celebrating the few that can afford to give. God is against such systems. The church of Jesus should have no boundary between the rich and the poor.

To the leaders, pastors and ministers, God is reminding them again in Acts 7:48-50: "However, the Most High doesn't live in temples (church) made by human hand. As the prophet says, "Heaven is my throne, and the earth is my footstool. Could you build me a temple (building) as good as that?" asks the Lord. "Could you build me such a resting place? Didn't my hands make both heaven and earth?" It is not proper to start meetings or services by saying "We welcome everybody to the house of God." It is far better to say "We welcome everybody to this fellowship or family meeting." The Bible says "For where two or three gather together as my followers (in my name) I am there among them" (Matthew 18:20). As leaders, we shall all stand before God, giving an account of the resources He has put in our hands. "Yes, each of us will give a personal account to God" (Romans 14:12).

If not a display of foolishness and a religious spirit, how do you build a dream structure and call it the House of God. No! We are the house of God, the temple where God dwells and not in the building that will be consumed by fire. Therefore, the church should invest in people more than structures. Beloved, don't be deceived; you are the temple of God. "And you are living stones that God is building into his spiritual temple. What's more, you are his holy priests. Through the mediation of Jesus Christ, you offer spiritual sacrifices that please God" (1 Peter 2:5).

Chapter Six

The Church: A House of Prayer

The Church prays so much and yet there is no lasting result, just because our prayers are manufactured by emotions.

"But you, dear friends, must build each other up in your most holy faith, pray in the power of the Holy Spirit…"

Jude 20

There are lots of words interchangeably used with the word Church, such as a temple, the assembly, called out, house of God and Zion. It has been clearly established that these words are context- based and really do not refer to an architectural structure, rather they speak of humans. This is why the prophet Isaiah declared by the spirit of God: "I will bring them to my holy mountain of Jerusalem and will fill them with joy in my house of prayer. I will accept their burnt offerings and sacrifices, because my Temple will be called a house of prayer for all nations." (Isaiah 56:7) Jesus also reaffirmed this in the scriptures. He said to them, "The scriptures declare, my temple will be called a house of prayer,' but you have turned it into a den of thieves!" (Matthew 21:13). Jesus is saying here, that one of the distinguishing features and functions of a true church is prayer. Therefore, we can safely assert that prayer should be the operating system of the church. Little wonder, the scriptures recall many times that Jesus separated himself for prayer. Luke 9:28 says, "About eight days later Jesus took Peter, James, and John up on a mountain to pray." If the place where Jesus went to pray with His disciples had been mentioned as a Temple instead of a mountain some people might have misunderstood it for a structure or a building.

It is clear that the concept of the Temple in the Old Testament context could no longer the mind of God in the new dispensation. In the Old Testament, prayer was expected to be done only in the Temple, where God's presence could only be guaranteed. Hannah's example paints this picture perfectly in I Samuel 1:9-11 when she was praying for child bearing. This could mean that men's confidence was in bringing their challenges to God at the temple where He could only be accessed then.

However, now, there is no boundary and limitation any longer as Jesus said: "But the time is coming- indeed, it's here now- when true worshipers will worship the father in spirit and in truth. The father is looking for those who worship him that way"

(John 4:23). It means, therefore, that prayer can actually take place anywhere and anytime. Location is no longer an issue and men don't need to go to a particular building, i.e. the temple, to meet with God because He now resides in us.

PRAYER

In the book, The Prayer Life, Wale Odeniyi defines prayer as a form of communication between God and man. He clarifies this position, saying that prayer is "the impression of the spirit in the human heart to bring about something from nothing." He continues by saying, "Prayer gives testimony to the resurrection of Jesus. It is an expression of divine intervention in human existence; to see the invisible, without considering the impossible." He also quoted E.M. Bound: "It is better to let the work go by default than to let prayer go by neglect." This means that prayer is a necessary condition for righteous living and particularly for anyone who wants to be in tune with God at all times.

I have found it very difficult to ascribe a particular definition or description to prayer. I see prayer as a supernatural energy, which can't be held, but its impact can be felt indisputably. I would be defining prayer on a functional and operational basis rather than on a definitive prescription. It is only relevant here on earth as there is nothing like prayer in heaven except praises unto our God. Therefore, I will proceed to define prayer according to the various encounters, manifestations and references of men.

PRAYER AS A MEDIUM OF COMMUNICATION

Throughout the scriptures, we see several situations where men expressed their hearts unto God and He in turn heard them either by warning them or granting absolute pardon. There can't be effective, communication without a clear message of understanding and language. Also, communication without feedback to the sender is not effective.

"If your people go out where you send them to fight their enemies, and if they pray to you by turning towards this city you have chosen, and toward this temple I have built to honor your name, then hear their prayers from heaven and uphold their cause." 2 Chronicles 6:4-5 (see also Numbers 21:4-9).

Prayer is a tested and dependable tool in the hands of men to relate with God. It is the ignition in our relationship with God. It provides the needed spark to keep the relationship alive. Little wonder Jesus lived a life of prayer all through His ministry on earth, even to the point of death. John 5:30 says:" I can do nothing on my own, I judge as God tells me. Therefore, my judgment is just, because I carry out the will of the one who sent me, not my own will." It is clear that the reason why the church is not in tune with heaven is that it is not praying as it ought to. How many saints, including you my dear reader, can speak the mind of God for your life, business, marriage, children and nation. It doesn't happen by accident. It comes in the place of prayer. A living church should have the capacity to speak and hear from God.

PRAYER AS A TOOL FOR DIVINE INTERVENTION

When we talk about intervention, it is an act of interference, involvement or stepping into a particular issue or case. Prayer as a tool for divine intervention simply means the power that brings heavenly assistance to us.

"Soon the people began to complain about their hardship, and the Lord heard everything they said, then the Lord's anger blazed against them, and he sent a fire to rage among them, and he destroyed some of the people in the outskirts of the camp. Then the people screamed to Moses for help, and when he prayed to the Lord, the fire stopped." Numbers11: 1-2 (See also Psalm 106:23).

"Around midnight Paul and Silas were praying and singing hymns to God, and the other prisoners were listening. Suddenly, there was a massive earthquake, and the prison was shaken to its foundations. All the doors immediately flew open, and the chains of every prisoner fell off! The Jailer woke up to see the prison doors wide open. He assumed the prisoners had escaped, so he drew his sword to kill himself. But Paul shouted to him, stop! Don't kill yourself! We are all here!" Acts 16:25-28

Beloved, God still needs a Moses that will intervene by pleading to God on behalf of the rebellious nations and the Church of God. The church in the wilderness quickly forgot the goodness of God and they began to complain. The deadness we are experiencing in the church today needs the intervention of the Moses's of our times. Where are they? What shall we say about Paul, who was very conscious of the potency of divine intervention and the faithfulness of God? A man of prayer would always bring down the hands of God in every hopeless situation. Paul and Silas are good examples of true churchmen whose voices carried weight in the realm of the spirit. They were not just having a ritual and a religious vigil of prayer and worship, but they had confidence in God and through their actions, many came to the knowledge of God. If only the church will pray, there shall never be any challenge that will be able to withstand us.

PRAYER IS THE KEY TO REVIVAL AND REFORMATION

There is a difference between revival and reformation. Revival is bringing to life that which was dead while reformation is carrying out a right restructuring or renovation that which is deformed, i.e. re-forming that which is deformed. There can't be a revival until the church does something. Until men are ready to travail and prevail in prayer, revival won't happen. The devil is fooling the church by encouraging her to organize crusades and meetings which are tagged as "revivals" No! God is the only one that can make true revival happen, and that will be after the church has prayed. Where there is a revival, the preacher doesn't need to preach so much; men will beg to give up their wicked ways and submit to the true God.

Revival is God walking in the streets. When this happens, the whole community will be swept by His power, such that there will be mass salvation and commitment. If the church will pray for revival, the results will start from the church; there will be no place for the deceiver in the body of Christ. The Bible recalls the impact of the incident that happened to Ananias and Sapphira in the early church:

"Great fear gripped the entire church and everyone else who heard what had happened." Acts 5: 11

That is not only the church, but as many that heard it feared the Lord. There was also another revival that broke out in the early church that was also documented in Acts of the Apostles.

"And an appointment with Herod was granted. When the day arrived, Herod put on his royal robes, sat on his throne, and made a speech to them" the people gave him a great ovation, shouting, "it's the voice of a god, not of a man! Instantly, an angle of the Lord struck Herod with a sickness, because he accepted the people's worship instead of giving the glory to God. So he was consumed with worms and died. Meanwhile, the word of God continued to spread, and there were many new believers." Acts 12:21-24

You can ask yourself this question, who preached to these new believers? This is the impact of revival. Are you prepared for revival? It is not in talking or preaching, it is in doing.

Reformation is reconfiguring that which is misshaped or deformed. Whatsoever that is deformed can never carry out its full functions properly. And reformation is more of internal than external. It is highly impossible for a deformed heart to bring about a reformed world. A deformed church will never be able to fix the problem of the deformed world. Reformation is not a function of information. Many organizations and Nations are dying seeking for messiah, even though the leaders are well informed. Yet they are helpless. The reason why it won't work is this: information comes from outside to inside, while reformation starts from within and then springs forth outside. It will take only the reformer, not the informer to change the situation for the better.

"....And do not conformed to this world, but be transformed by the renewing of your mind, that you may prove what is that good and acceptable and perfect will of God" Romans 12:2NKJ.

This can only happen by constant prayer and living by the word of God. Until this happens, a man will find it difficult to live acceptably perfect, and living to please according to His will for others to see and follow. Until the church becomes transformed or reformed, she can't be a model for the world to follow. It is not in confession or mere slogan, it actually goes beyond that.

PRAYER: THE KEY THAT UNLOCKS REVELATION.

Revelations are secrets or mysteries of the divinity that are revealed to humanity. Revelation is a product of the Holy Spirit's information and not a product of brain-work. Revelations are hidden truths that God releases or downloads into the hearts of men. It is very easy for a man of prayer to tap into the mind of God. One of the reasons why the present church is failing compared to the early church is the issue of our inability to see beyond ordinary. A man that cannot see Is like an eagle that flies at the same altitude with other birds.

A church that can see well will not waste resources on trial and error programs. It will not compete with others and her energy would be preserved. A believer's life becomes better if he can see ahead of time because nothing will catch him unawares. This is the level that the church is supposed to be operating at. This is the basis on which you can identify the true church. "Jesus replied, you are blessed, Simon, son of John, because my father in heaven has revealed this to you. You did not learn this from any human being. Now I say to you that you are Peter (which means rock), and upon this rock (revelation) I will build my church, and all the power of hell will not conquer it." (Matthew 16:17-18). When revelation is out of the church, it becomes dead. Peter was able to speak that which no man had taught him as it came to him from the spirit realm. "When the servant of the man of God got up early the next morning and went outside, there were troops, horses, and chariots everywhere. "Oh, sir, what will we do now? The young man cried to Elisha. Don't be afraid! Elisha told him. For there are more on our side than on theirs! Then Elisha prayed, O Lord, open his eyes and let him see! The Lord opened the young man's eyes and when he looked up, he saw that the hillside around Elisha was filled with horses and chariots of fire." (2 Kings 6: 15-17)

Thank God that prophet Elisha could see, otherwise his servant would definitely have prevented him from gaining speed because they weren't seeing the same thing. He prayed unto God for his inner eyes to be opened and God did as Elisha requested. Many pastors and leaders cannot see today, how do you want to lead right, and gain speed? How do you want to control your flock? Prayer is one of the dynamic tools that grant men access to revelation. There can never be a true church without revelation, and there can never be revelation without a life of prayer. Prophetic direction comes through a life of prayer.

PRAYER ALIGNS MEN'S HEARTS TO THE WILL OF GOD.

When we talk about the will of God, we are referring to the exact purpose or picture in His mind for every issue. God is spirit and not a man; it will take His Spirit in man to download His very mind of God. It does not matter how careful a man may be, if he cannot pick the mind of God per time it will be very impossible to please God. My prayer for you is that you will understand the mind of God per time. Friends, one grace I enjoy in God is that nothing takes me by surprise. He speaks and reveals things to me ahead of time and this is the best experience a man can have in Him. I desire a higher dimension because I am not satisfied with my current level. Any saint that cannot hear or understand the plans of God for himself and at least his immediate family and community is dead. This has nothing to do with the position you are occupying within your local assembly.

"Once, after a sacrificial meal at Shiloh, Hannah got up and went to pray. Eli the priest was sitting at his customary place beside the entrance of the tabernacle. Hannah was in deep anguish, crying bitterly as she prayed to the Lord. And she made this vow, O Lord of Heaven's Armies, if you will look upon my sorrow and answer my prayer and give me a son, then I will give him back to you. He will be yours for his entire life time, and as a sign that he has been dedicated to the Lord, his hair will never be cut." I Samuel 1: 9-11

"Also, I asked the Lord to give me this boy, and he has granted my request. Now I am giving him to the Lord, and he will belong to the Lord his whole life and they worshiped the Lord there." Samuel 1:27-28

Friends, God has a need at every point in time. At this point He needed a prophet in the land of Israel since Eli and his two children had missed the mark and ruined the ministry for themselves and their family. The Bible records that the word of God was very scarce in Israel, because nobody knew how to download the mind of God for the nation.

Hannah needed a son for her reproach (barrenness) to be removed, and God also needed a prophet that would give direction to the nation. Hannah prayed right for the first time by aligning her desire with the will of God. A true church is one that has no personal ambition, but the vision God reveals. Friends, the will of God is still hanging, will you agree to partner with Him in meeting His will? He is looking for saints like Hannah. Until we begin to pray His mind, we shall be wasting our time. The man that knows how to pray is not the man with a long prayer, but a man that can demand or pray for that which concerns God the most.

Another way by which you can identify men who are running their own lives and ambition is by greed. They are only good at collecting. They can't give back to God what he has given to them. Abraham gave Isaac from his heart. May I not receive the blessing, which I will find difficult to give back to God. Beloved, there is nothing that you have which you didn't receive from the Lord. Is it money, beauty, fame, position, intelligence? It is also out of what He has released that we have received and out of what we have received that we have gathered. Ask yourself, what do I have that I can't give back to God? "He went on a little farther and bowed with his face to the ground praying, my father! If it is possible, let this cup of suffering be taken away from me. Yet I want your will to be done, not mine." (Matthew 26:39). Jesus had a desire in his heart, but allowed the will of the Father to take prominence. Until we get to this level, we would not be able to conquer the enemy. The power and enablement are released in the place of prayer. Pray and pray today.

PRAYER, THE PLATFORM FOR INTERCESSION

In the Old Testament, one of the duties of a priest was intercession. What does it mean to intercede? It is speaking persuasively on behalf of a guilty person. It is standing in between two parties and making a plea for mercy on behalf of one party.

"Soon the people began to complain about their hardship, and the Lord heard everything they said. Then the Lord's anger blazed against them, and he sent a fire to rage among them, and he destroyed some of the people in the outskirts of the camp. Then the people screamed to Moses for help, and when he prayed to the Lord, the fire stopped." Numbers 11: 1-2

God respects the voice of the Church. If it is sensitive enough to take responsibility for her world, God's mercy will be released. Sometimes our brethren, even ministers, fall short of the standard of God; instead of the church to intercede, that person becomes a laughing stock and a subject of mockery while the devil rejoices. It is by the grace of God that we are standing. Let us cry unto God on behalf of those who are misbehaving. In the New Testament, Christ brought us into the position of priesthood and one of the duties of a priest is to stand in the gap and make up the hedge so that the serpent won't be able to bite. When God wanted to destroy Jericho, He told Abraham. And Abraham pleaded and gave reasons to God that Jericho should be preserved. Jesus interceded for Peter when the devil wanted to have him: "Simon, Simon, Satan has asked to sift each of you like wheat. But I have pleaded in prayer for you, Simon, that your faith should not fail. So when you have repented and turned to me again, strengthen your brothers." (Luke 22:31-32) Let us learn the art of intercession, especially for our leaders and servants of God, because they are very susceptible to attacks.

PRAYER BRINGS PROPHETIC DIRECTION.

A sense of direction is one of the attributes that should separate the church from the confusion in the world today. Nothing should meet us unawares and if it does happen, it shouldn't bring us into confusion because we have the mind of Christ. A sense of direction should be the hallmark of any genuine child of God. We won't talk about the will of the Father, if the direction is not clear. God spoke to Moses many times as he led the church of God through the wilderness. How do you want to avoid without misbehaving in your own wilderness, if you cannot hear God, to receive a clear direction? Your home, business, ministry and decisions shouldn't be a product of professional consultants, but by the leading of God. Where are the professionals in these days of economic meltdown? They too have been meltdown; their ideologies have failed, but God can never fail. When the church begins to place primacy on prayer, there will be a clear direction instead of delusion and confusion.

PRAYER PRECEDES POWER

There is a common saying: a prayerless Christian is a powerless Christian. We live our lives to pray, then we pray to live. Prayer is soaring on the wings of the spirit until humanity is brought to a place of divinity. The true church of Jesus was built on power and unreserved authority. It is this power and authority that put the church in charge of world affairs. "...He replied, "The father alone has the authority to set those dates and times and they are not for you to know. But you will receive power when the Holy Spirit comes upon you. And you will be my witness, telling people about me everywhere in Jerusalem, throughout Judea, in Samaria and to the ends of the earth" Acts 1:7-8

But many people who heard their message believed it. So the number of believers now totaled about 5,000 men, not counting women and the children. The next day, the council of all the rulers and elders and teachers of religious law met in Jerusalem. Annas the high priest was there along with Caiaphas John, Alexander, and others relatives of the high priest. They brought in the two disciples and demand, "By what power, or in whose name, have you done this? Then Peter, filled with the Holy Spirit, said to them, "Rulers and elders of our people, are we being questioned today because we've done a good deed for a crippled man? Do you want to know how he was healed? Let me clearly state to all of you, all the people of Israel that he was healed by the powerful name of Jesus Christ the Nazarene, the man you crucified but whom God raised from the dead. Acts 4:5-10

From the scriptures above, it will be known to you that there is no substitute for the power of the church. The early church was so powerful to the extent that 5,000 men accepted their message in one day. The question is how did the early apostles do it? How did they communicate clearly and loudly to the multitude without any public address system? Also, these apostles were illiterate men, crude and unrefined, standing up to address the top echelon of the nation without any iota of fear. This is an exhibition of the power of God through the Holy Spirit. Peter was filled with the Holy Spirit; many people, including the leaders of today's church, are filled up with different kinds of spirit.

"Your people shall be volunteers (willingly) in the day of your power..." Psalm 110:3

There can't be a church without the power of the Holy Ghost.

PRAYER IS THE STAMP OF THE CHURCH

A stamp is a mark that confirms originality and approval. For example, the international passport carries a visa on which a stamp is embossed; this gives you access into that country. When we say that prayer is a tool of approval, the Bible says "And I will give you the keys of the kingdom of Heaven. Whatever you forbid on earth will be forbidden in heaven, and whatever you permit on earth will be permitted in heaven." (Matthew 16:19). "I tell you, you can pray for anything and if you believe that you've received it, it will be yours." (Mark 13: 24) When the church, God's representative on earth, declares a thing, heaven would back-up that request. Heaven is waiting for your call. We can also look at prayer as an earthly license for a heavenly intervention. God loves order and principles; He will never break His word.

An official promissory note that carries an authorized stamp is equivalent to having cash at hand. However, you can only cash that note on the counter of belief. We must believe that we carry authority, i.e. the stamp that can give us, heavenly attention and access. Every genuine believer has a stamp to validate documents for heavenly release. When two believers agree or pray concerning any matter, they are stamping the issue with two stamps. The more stamps, the more authentic and valid the document is. This is the basic operating principle behind the prayer of agreement. It is very painful that the church today has lost the true essence of its stamp. While some who have the original are using it wrongly and for selfish reasons, others carry fake stamps like the seven sons of Sceva, who was using the name of Jesus to operate a fake deliverance ministry. See Acts 19:13-16. The question is: what kind of stamp are you carrying, original or imitation? If it is original, what are you really using it for? "And even when you ask, you don't get it because ye ask amiss, that ye may consume it upon your lusts"

(James 2:1). Let's be frank, of what purpose is the visa stamp on the cover page of a travelling passport? Though it's a genuine visa if it is not on the right page, it is useless, access to the desired country will not be granted.

A dead church is not only one that doesn't pray, but one that is praying wrongly as the scriptures above tells us. Our prayer meetings today are full of selfish desires and items called prayer points. Haven't you discovered that even some local assemblies and denominations are praying for God to elevate them above others, so that their own voice will sound louder in the land? Little wonder that the church is becoming weaker. Until the spirit of Babylon, the competitive spirit, is judged in the church, achieving unity may be difficult and saving our community may be impossible. This is because we are not ready to agree on stamping the right page together for the release of Heaven. If all we seek

God's power and authority for is to get our needs met, it's not worth all the trouble. Prayer, the stamp of the church, must be used rightly.

JESUS' PATTERN OF PRAYER

Jesus gathered His disciples to teach them how to pray at a particular point in time (Matthew 6:9-13). Knowing full well that many pray, but it's just showmanship, a form of entertainment, or gymnastic activity like the Pharisees. So for them not to labor in vain, thinking they were praying, he taught them how they could receive heavenly attention. This is what we call the Lord's Prayer today. This is a pattern that should guide believers while praying.

Our Father in Heaven, may your name be kept...

When we pray as a church, i.e. the called out ones, we should be conscious that our citizenship is not of this world because our Father is in Heaven. Therefore, we should always be conscious of this relationship. Also, we must not forget that His name deserves honor, worship, and adoration. Our fathers in time past related with His name and things He did for them. Jehovah Tsidkenu, He is the Lord our righteousness. (Jeremiah 23:6), Jehovah Shalom Jehovah our peace (Judges 6:23-24) Jehovah M'Keddesh - Lord who sacrifices (1Cor 6: 11);

Jehovah Shammah, Jehovah is here (Ezekiel 48:35);

Jehovah Rophe, Jehovah heals (Exodus 15:26);

Jehovah Jireh, Jehovah our provider (Genesis 22:4);

Jehovah Nissi, Jehovah our captain (Exodus 17:15);

Jehovah Rohi, Jehovah our shepherd. (Psalm 23:1).

May your kingdom come soon. May your will be done on earth as it is in heaven.

Jesus is teaching here that when you are to pray or ask for anything, it must be a thing that pertains to the Kingdom of God. We are to pray for God's ruling system to come down to the earth. When his kingdom comes upon our affairs, community, organization or nation, it would be sweet. When we say, t "Let your will be done on earth." What we are saying is that we are here on earth as your delegates and we are not running our own agenda but His alone we shall be forever. It will be very difficult for a man to be demanding for God's will without knowing God or having a personal relationship with Him else every of your desire while praying would be to please yourself. And this is not a signpost for a true church. As a church we must get to the point, where our will would align with the will of God. I don't mean our will should look like His own, but exactly His own. Therefore, check those prayer points again. Are they for self-gratification or to His glory?

Give us today the food we need.

Jesus wants us to exercise a high level of trust in the Father, believing that our needs can be met through Him alone. God wants us to live our lives everyday, trusting Him. This is the highest expression of our trust in the Lord. He provided manna and quails for the church in the wilderness daily. He didn't allow them to store it for another day. The parable of the Rich Fool in Luke 12:13-21, whose business yielded so much that he couldn't handle it and when he looked at his bank accounts and assets, he told himself, "O boy You have what it takes to eat the best for the rest of your life." He didn't recognize the place of his Maker, who gave him the power to make wealth. However, on that same day when he was making the decision to restructure his business empire, God required his life from him.

Among many things, Jesus said in teaching this parable there are two statements that struck my heart.

a. Then he said, "Beware! Guard against every kind of greed. Life is not measured by how much you own."

b. "Yes, a person is a fool to store up earthly wealth, but not have a rich relationship with God" (Luke 12:15-21).

This is why brethren in some assemblies are storing up for unborn generations when they are personally satisfied, while other people in the congregation very close to them have no shelter or even what to eat. This is the spirit of the world, now fully in control of many churches. Even shepherds are eating the best of the best while their flocks are dying. Is this a sign of breakthrough? All unrighteousness shall be judged. Surprisingly, even those in the occults are showing themselves love and more affection than the church of Jesus Christ. Apostle Paul says, "And I trust that my life will bring honor to Christ, whether I live or die for to me, living means living for Christ, and dying is even better." (Philippians 1: 20-21). Many believers are living for themselves, not for Christ. We have now converted God's grace for personal use. This is very disheartening.

And forgive us our sins, as we have forgiven those who sin against us.

It is possible to pray and there will still be hindrances. Some of these are bitterness and unforgiving spirit, which are a form of poison dwelling inside some brethren. They are killing spirits. Such were the spirits in operation in the life of Cain. We easily ask for forgiveness of our sins from God our Father, but we don't easily forgive our brothers and sisters In the Lord. Where did we pick up this nature, if truly we are of the Father? Jesus wants us to love; this is the true nature of God. Love does not keep the records of wrongs.

When Peter asked Jesus ion a question the subject of forgiveness, the Master was assertive in declaring: "No, not seven times" "But seventy times seven!" (Matthew 18:22) The calculation Jesus gave was 490 times. If this nature of God is in you, you can't have a storage facility for bitterness. No man can offend you 490 times daily, even if he takes it to be a full- time job. Friends, it doesn't matter what that fellow has done to wrong you; because of the love of Jesus who died for all of us that fellow must be forgiven.

This is why we spent much time in prayer, but there is no result. These are the weapons, which the enemy is using against us.

And don't let us yield to temptation, but rescue us from the evil one.

Every temptation comes from the devil and aimed at ensuring that we don't meet the standard of God. We are prone to temptation on a daily basis by what we see, touch, hear, taste and smell, but God has given you the grace to live above this. Also, every day comes with its own challenges, so it is very important to recognize that our strength to conquer is not in our big muscles, but in God. Even Jesus, the Son of God, was tempted but He did not sin, although Adam also was tempted and he fell. Every temptation we encounter as children of God is to take us to the next level in God. Also, don't forget that the evil one's job is to see you fall, but by praying unto God with the right attitude and spirit, His grace and power will be released and you will be victorious.

For the Kingdom is yours, the power and the Glory forever.

We would see from the pattern of Jesus' prayer that as we come before our Father, we should lay down our problems and challenges by praising His holy name. After we have made our requests known to Him; we should also adore Him for He is the ruler of the Kingdom. The entire powers that be and the glory belong to Him. This gives us comfort that what we have prayed for has been answered.

WHEN THE CHURCH PRAYS

The church is endowed with much authority that can only be activated through prayer and revelation knowledge of our God. The early church was able to turn the world upside down for Christ because they did not relent in prayer. I have heard many say that everything is not prayer, but for the true church, it's everything! Though one mustn't do the wrong thing and believe that prayer will correct the error.

"Afterward, when Jesus was alone in the house with his disciples, they asked him, Why couldn't we cast out that evil spirit?" Jesus replied, "This kind can be cast out only by prayer…" Mark 9:28-29

If Jesus could hold this position on prayer, why then do we try to substitute prayer with other things? Herod Agrippa was persecuting the early church.

"About that time King Herod Agrippa began to persecute some believers in the church. He had the apostle James (John's brother) killed with a sword. When Herod saw how much this pleased the Jewish people, he also arrested Peter. (This took place during the Passover celebration) Then he imprisoned him, placing him under the guard of four squads of four soldiers each. Herod intended to bring Peter out for public trial after the Passover. But while Peter was in prison, the church prayed very earnestly for him" Acts 12:1-4

The death of James Zebedee was orchestrated by Herod Agrippa, but endorsed by the church. You might ask, how? Jesus said whatsoever the church permits to happen on earth will be permitted in heaven. By extension, the church has the final say on everything on earth and not the head of any nation like King Herod. The church can cancel the policies of the ruling parties and governments that do not align with God purposes. The church is the true ruling party endowed with power and authority on earth. If the church had decided to cancel and frustrate the activities of Herod at that time, heaven would have overthrown the plans. But the church quickly went to pray when they discovered that Peter was next in line. When the church prayed, heaven intervened and the prison guards were replaced and sentenced to death by Herod for allowing Peter to leave the prison, but actually the angel of God broke the chains and locks of the prison gates. The potency of the church lies in the power of prayer.

Why are the nation's rulers embezzling, misappropriating and looting the national treasury and the church is doing nothing about it. Analyzing the issue would not stop Herod from destroying lives and visions, but when we take our place in the spirit, we can stop the hand of every Herod of our generation.

The reason the world has not submitted to our God is that the church is playing instead of praying. Our assemblies are now centers of entertainment. We are raising holy and refined men and women who speak grammatically with the devil. Daniel prayed and the whole nation submitted to his God. If nothing has happened in the lives of men and women around you in your many years of salvation, you are a disgrace to the Kingdom, a debtor who is wasting the grace of God. You are like the fig tree without fruits; when demand will be placed on you, what will you tell your Maker? Will you receive an axe or a curse to dry up? The decision is yours.

The impact of the church is little or no longer felt, as it were, though denominational assemblies are springing up and large crowds are gathering at meetings. The sad reality is that our camps have become leper colonies; the assemblies of the Gehazis. Today, discernment is no more in the church as we are celebrating the growth of our personal empires called churches, which are filled with the Ananias's, Sapphiras, Gehazis and even the sons of Scevas of this world. These groups of people would end up bringing shame to their managers or the so-called pastors.

The ministry of prayer must be restored if our lives and the world will ever experience any change that will bring glory to our God. History can be changed or made on our knees. The man who kneels before God can stand up to anything. Jesus said His house should be called the house of prayer. You and I should be carriers of the authority and power if God is truly resident in our inside.

PREPARE FOR WAR

What is war? It is a situation in which two or more parties are engaged in a fight over a period of time over a particular issue(s). Some of the many reasons that cause wars include competitive will, dominance and superiority complex. Warfare employs the use of particular weapons or methods, such as biological warfare, nuclear and chemical warfare, tactical warfare, and spiritual warfare. Among these forms of warfare, the spiritual warfare is the most ferocious and the strongest of all. It is beyond human sophistry. It is highly prophetic. Even nuclear weapons cannot withstand its high capacity for efficacy. When Elijah locked up the economy of Israel for three and a half years, there were no means of national livelihood. There was nothing men could do at that juncture than to submit and surrender to the power of heaven. Such is the kind of power available in spiritual warfare. In this kind of warfare, you don't need to carry any physical ammunition. It was this same kind of weapon that David used against Goliath. They are not popular and make no sense to the human faculty, but they are very dependable.

"We are human, but we don't wage war as humans do. We use God's might weapons, not worldly weapons, to knock down the strongholds of human reasoning and to destroy false arguments. We destroy every proud obstacle that keeps people from knowing

God. We capture their rebellious thoughts and teach them to obey Christ. (2 Corinthians: 10:3-5).

This also means that the time for religious living is long gone. Jehovah is a man of war. He is referred to as the Lord of hosts, many times in the scripture. He can't be a Lord of hosts, if he doesn't engage in battle. Daniel saw a vision thousands of years ago that makes this picture clearer.

"I Daniel was troubled by all I had seen, and my visions terrified me... as I watched, this horn was waging war against God's holy people and was defeating them, until the Ancient One the Most High- came and judged in favor of his holy people. Then the time arrived for the holy people to take over the Kingdom...." (Daniel 7:15-28).

If God, our Father, is a Man of War, who are you then to say that you are seeking peace by your human understanding. Demons and their master, the devil, do not understand dialogue or any vocabulary other than violence. The enemy does not want you to fulfill the purpose for which you were created. The accurate will of God for your life is a threat to the enemy. How then will you live to please God and do His will without warfare? It is just a sheer waste of time not to be battle ready. Every believer must engage in warfare. Warfare is not just shouting while praying. It is a concept of warring with revelation knowledge. It is the ability to understand the will of God per time and be willing to partner with heaven on earth to bring to fruition the plans and purpose of God, by dislodging the trespasser, the enemy of our soul.

DECLARING WAR

It takes a prophetic man to declare a war and it takes an apostolic might to wage the war. A man that cannot see what is wrong will not be able to declare a war against such wickedness in high places. Negotiation and reason can never put the enemy under subjection. Adam was insensitive by allowing reasoning to take the place of the accurate word of God and so he bought the idea of the devil in the garden, thus losing all. Take note of this: there is no way you can work accurately in the will of God and be involved in kingdom advancement on earth without being a man or woman of war.

The devil's agenda is to see his kingdom in charge of the operations on this side of eternity. Will you and I fold our arms by our complacency and religious spirit and watch the enemy take over our Father's kingdom? No! When Jesus was teaching His disciples on how to pray, what do you think was in His mind when he prayed, "May your Kingdom come." He was implicitly saying that you must keep on declaring war against every contrary kingdom. No kingdom can be established without a fight.

Jesus said "And from the time John the Baptist began preaching until now, the kingdom of heaven has been forcefully advancing, and violent people are attacking it." Matthew 11:12

There are key expressions to be carefully looked at in the scriptures above. First, "The Kingdom of Heaven" which talks about the rulership of God on earth as it is in exact operation in heaven. Second, "Forcefully advancing" which talks about breakthrough or penetrating an area without permission or seeking the opinion of someone before doing so. It means violating the norms. Then "violent" which talks about aggressiveness, warring or fighting. This implies that no man can be a true ambassador of this kingdom without being a fighter. Even Apostle Paul, while admonishing Timothy, says, "Timothy, my son, here are my instructions for you, based on prophetic words about you earlier. May they help you fight well in the Lord's battles." (I Timothy 1:18).

How many of us are ready to lay down our lives to see God's kingdom established and see His will rule here on earth. This is the desire of God, but fighters and warriors are needed. John, the Beloved caught a revelation and declared: "Then the seventh angel blew his trumpet and there were loud voices shouting in heaven: "The world has now become the Kingdom of our Lord and of his Christ and he will reign forever and ever" (Rev 11:15). This great revelation was a picture of the end, but for it to come to pass, we must all be engaged in spiritual warfare against hell and its allied forces.

May the grace to fight, ability to see far, wisdom to strategize and the revelation knowledge of God be imparted to you in Jesus name. You are the house of God and His house shall be called "the house of prayer for all nations."

Chapter Seven

The Church: In The World

"One of the ways to measure a true church is when her constructive impact is felt at least within her immediate environment. The true church is not designed to exploit men, but to raise kingdom citizens."

"The Spirit of the Lord is upon me, for He has anointed me to bring Good News to the poor. He has sent me to proclaim that captives will be released, that the blind will see, that the oppressed will be set free, and that the time of the Lord's favor has come."

Luke 4:18-19

The definition of the church can never be overemphasized. This will put us on the right track. Church refers to a set of people with a sense of direction and purpose, separated for a specific or defined assignment. Every call is for a definite purpose. When a man says God called him and he cannot say in a statement his purpose of being called; he is merely being emotional, taking up a responsibility that was not given to him.

Church also means the assembly, i.e. the established and constitutionally set-up body to be at the helm of affairs of the world. As an assembly, it also means the highest constituted body, such as the senate of some nations. This means that the church can never be of this world, but from God. When we are talking about the 'world', we are referring to the general operational system of the universe, which the church was originally designed to be in charge of and manage. We can see from the account of creation in Genesis 1:1-25 how God created the heavens and the earth, including everything that exist today, excluding man. It was after God had created everything that he decided to make man in His own image so as to be like Him. (Genesis1: 26). The church was not created for the world, but the world (earth) was created for the church to control.

"The one who comes from above is above all; the one who is of the earth belongs to the earth and speaks about earthly things. The one who comes from heaven is above all." John 3:10

This was actually the position and the state of man until he fell, but thank God for Jesus who restored us to this place of primacy with God. The church is the offspring of God. Lion can only give birth to a lion, Goat to goat, and God to gods. No wonder God says to Moses, "...Pay close attention to this, I will make you seem like God to Pharaoh, and your brother, Aaron, will be your prophet." (Exodus 7:1).

The Church is actually expected to be God on earth over everything, including unbelievers, who don't have the nature of God but have imbibed the system of the world. "For whatever is born of God overcomes the world. And this is the victory that has overcome the world-our faith" (1 John 5:4). The church actually came out of the life of God. Therefore, we shouldn't exhibit anything different from the life of the Father here on earth.

A painful fact, today is that the church is in competition in the world. The system of this world has almost become the standard for the church, mention any area of life: education, fashion, finance, business, management, marriage, etc. As a matter of fact the world is dictating the pace for the church. What a great error and abuse of purpose!

It will be very difficult for the church to get it right until her allegiance is given to Jesus, until we begin to take our purpose beyond ourselves, until we embrace the power of oneness, recognizing that we are one body, living for a singular kingdom with only one King. Why do we subject to the spirit of competition and self-acclamation? If the church is going to shape the world, it must first get it right within before looking outside to rescue the world.

THE CHURCH AND THE DYING WORLD

The church as the representative of God on earth is not a puppet, dummy or figurehead, neither is it a ceremonial personality but an active and powerful entity with great responsibility.

"Don't you believe that I am in the father and the father is in me? The words I speak are not my own, but my father who lives in me does his work through me. Just believe that I am in the father and the father is in me. Or, at least believe because of the work you have seen me do. I tell you the truth, anyone who believes in me will do the same works I have done and even greater works, because I am going to be with the father. You can ask for anything in my name, and I will do it, so that the son can bring glory to the father." John 14: 10-13

Jesus and the Father are one, going by the analogy above. He lives in the Father and the Father lives in Him. Jesus did great works. What are these great works? He opened the eyes of the blind, the lame walked, the sick were healed. He taught men proverbs, parables and words of wisdom for daily living. These are essential factors in the educational and orientation processes of a nation.

He fed multitudes and through them the word of God was activated, igniting the supernatural enablement within. He did not only teach on marriage, but also was involved in sweetening marriages. He restored the hopelessness of the people that was beyond the love and the consolation any man could give. Peter, a professional fisherman spent all night fishing, but he caught nothing until be met with Jesus. Interestingly, the Bible records that he needed not travel very far for his breakthrough, but that he was sorrowfully packing up his tools at the same place, where the Saviour changed his storyline. Can you imagine the number of people Peter would have hired the number of people that would have taken fish home for themselves and their families. Imagine the amount of money that would have gone to Peter's bank account after the sales. Look at the long run impact and effect on the people and the nation at large.

Jesus said, "The works that I did, greater shall the church do." Jesus was a family friend of Mary and Martha of Bethany, the sisters of Lazarus. Lazarus was very sick and died. His sisters sent for Jesus for a quick intervention. However, Jesus was not readily available.

"But when Jesus heard about it, he said, "Lazarus's sickness will not end up in death. No, it happened for the glory of God so that the son of God will receive the glory from this" John 11:4.

When He decided to go and attend to the Lazarus' case, He informed His disciples who discouraged him because of the problems they encountered at Judea before.

"Jesus replied, "There are twelve hours of daylight every day, during the day people can walk safely. They can see because they have the light of this world. But at night there is danger of stumbling because they have no light". Then he said, "Our friend Lazarus has fallen asleep, but now I will go and wake him" John11: 9-11.

The disciples said to Jesus, "Master, why are you disturbing yourself. Since he is sleeping, he would wake up at the right time." They didn't understand that what He was actually saying was that Lazarus was dead. He refused to address the situation the way it presented itself, but according to the power which was within Him. So He told them plainly, "Lazarus is dead and for your sakes, I'm glad I wasn't there, for now you will really believe. Come, let's go see him" John 11:14-15.

When Jesus arrived at Bethany, He was told that Lazarus was already in the grave, but when Martha heard that He was around, she went out to meet Him. She said, "Lord, if you had been around, my brother would not have died. But all the same you can ask God anything and they will do it for you."

To cut the story short, Jesus asked where Lazarus was buried and He was taken there. He asked that the stone at the tomb be rolled away.

"But Martha, the dead man's (Lazarus) sister, protested, Lord, he has been dead for four days. The smell will be terrible. Jesus responded, didn't I tell you that you would see God's glory if you believe? So they rolled the stone aside. Then Jesus looked up to heaven and said, Father, thank you for hearing me. You always hear me, but I say it out loud for the sake of all these people standing here, so that they will believe you sent me. Then Jesus shouted, Lazarus, come out! And the dead man came out, his hands and feet bound in grave clothes, his face wrapped in a head cloth. Jesus told them, unwrap him and let him go!" John 11: 39-44.

We can liken the deadness of Lazarus to the hopeless situation of the world. However, in the midst of all these pains and confusion, the true church has the solution and not the professionals. Jesus lives in the Father and the Father lives in Him. We are the structure that houses Jesus here on earth. We are the carriers of the divine nature of Jesus. Why then are we not manifesting anything close to what He did while He was here on earth? Not to talk of the greater works that He is still expecting from the real church that will emerge. Jesus declared His mission on earth openly and very early even before embarking on His earthly ministry by reading that which had been written concerning him:

"The Spirit of the Lord is upon me, for he has anointed me to bring Good News to the poor. He has sent me to proclaim that captives will be released, that the blind will see, that the oppressed will be set free, and that the time of the Lord's favor has come" Luke 4:18-19

Jesus actually performed all the things mentioned in His mission statement. Is the church today not actually disappointing God? Everything Jesus listed in His manifesto was about solving problems, the problems of humanity. No-one was pointed at Him. It is better for you and I to cross check this against the hidden tone of our personal vision and mission. If it does not bring absolute glory to God, it is a man made vision and mission and will never impact the world rightly. The church needs to take full responsibility for impacting the world. This is the essence of our being here on earth.

THE CHURCH AS A ROLE MODEL

One of the major mandates given to the church is to showcase the glory of our King to the earth by living right, thereby teaching the world. Preaching alone is not the best way to create impact, but by doing and teaching it.

"In my first book (Gospel of Luke) I told you, Theophilus, about everything Jesus began to do and teach" Acts 1:1

Luke the apostle emphasized the fact that Jesus did not first teach before doing rather He did and then taught. It is not how anointed you are in speech or preaching that counts, but how much of God in your speech. It is impossible for the church to be living wrong and expect a right lifestyle from the world. The church Jesus would be coming back for will be a model church with high standards of righteousness and kingdom value.

"In the last days, the mountain of the Lord's house will be the highest of all- the most important place on earth. It will be raised above the other hills (religions, philosophies and falsehood in churches), and people from all over the world will stream there to worship. People from many nations will come and say, "Come, let us go up to the mountains of the Lord, to the house of Jacob's God. There he will teach us his ways, and we will walk in his paths" for the Lord's teaching will go out from Zion; his word will go out from Jerusalem" (Isaiah 2: 2-3).

The question to ask ourselves is: when will this prophecy come to pass? When would the world seek the God of the church? When will they be looking for us for direction and instructions and ready to walk in the way of Truth? At this point, the management principles that will run organizations and nations will come from within the church, but before then, the church must excel and get it right. Then the world will come to live by the instructions of Zion (the church).

The world will never follow a corrupt church. The transparency of the church shall be seen, then men will submit themselves to God. Therefore, for the church to fulfill her purpose, there is a need for it to live up to the expectations of heaven. Dear friend, ask yourself these questions: How am I living my life on a daily basis? Can the world be changed for good by the reason of my lifestyle?

Chapter Eight

Beware of The Synagogue of Satan

"The potency in the Kingdom is not measured only by the size of man's world, but by the weight and impact of its life."

"You are the light of the world like a city on a hilltop that cannot be hidden. No one lights a lamp and is placed on a stand, where it gives light to everyone in the house"

Matthew 5:14-15

The word synagogue from the original Greek word synagogue means a "congregation". As used in the New Testament, it is referred to as a place of worship. The use of the synagogue is very common with the Jews, especially when they were not so large in number to build a solid structure, and there is a need for them to have a meeting place to worship, pray and read the Torah. The alternative for very devout Jews at that time was within the walls of the synagogue. "The same thing happened in Iconium. Paul and Barnabas went to the Jewish Synagogue and preached with such power that a great number of both Jews and Greeks became believers" (Acts 14:1).

Synagogue also means the assemblage of persons, a congregation, the meeting of a particular set of people. Therefore, it can be said to be an assembly of a particular set of people with a common goal. The assembly or could be godly or ungodly. This is exemplified in Acts 19:32-39. It is not every synagogue that is a gathering of God's people. It is not every worship center that is of God. It follows then that any congregation that is not of God will definitely be of the devil. There can never be a neutral ground.

Some people will say, "I don't have a religion. I'm a free thinker." There is no such thing like a free thinker. There is a spirit in you. If the Holy Spirit does not regenerate it, it is still in sin. The Bible also says, "He that sins is of the devil." No man can be a child of God without passing through a process of the new birth. Godly men gather to worship God in a synagogue. Satanists also gather to worship Satan in their own synagogue. Little wonder this was revealed to John, the Beloved, In the Revelation: "I know about your suffering and your poverty- but you are rich! I know the blasphemy of those opposing you. They say they are Jews, but they are not, because their Synagogue belongs to Satan" (Rev. 2:9).

What defines you as a church of God is not your outward appearance or the size of the congregation you belong. What separates the true synagogue of God from that of Satan is firstly the state of worshippers' hearts, their belief system and philosophy. God is a spirit and the only way He can be reached and worshiped is only in the spirit.

"But the time is coming - indeed, it's here now-when the true worshipers will worship the father in spirit and in truth. The father is looking for those who will worship him that way." John 4:23

One major characteristic of the synagogue of Satan is idolatry. They have built doctrines that support their gullibility. Most of them have exchanged materialism for true prosperity. Prosperity is truly part of the redemption package, but prosperity is bigger than money. It is the wholesomeness of God's grace over a man's life. The church has forgotten that men were not created for material and ephemeral things or for of material acquisition and enjoyment. These things were provided for us to achieve our primary aim on earth. They are tools. We are not living for them, but they are available for us because they were actually created for us as instruments to achieve our God- given vision on earth.

The message of the church has become imbalanced today because of the poverty and other challenges which the devil has clothed us with. We end up using our whole life thinking about money and our personal life aspirations. How many people today think of you as a representative of God's Kingdom in your office. Have you ever considered that your salary, which is motivating you to work, should be a secondary factor? Have you ever imagined that you have been sent to that office to actually make a difference, bring about change and leave behind the King's values and your kingdom legacy?

We should be exemplary apostles of God, sent to represent the interest of His kingdom in that establishment, rather than pollute ourselves and imbibe wrong values. "Whatsoever we do should be as unto the Lord." I am very conscious of the fact that there is no establishment that can pay me enough to quantify my worth and value. I am a carrier of God and His grace. What I have inside me is priceless. Everywhere I find myself, it is a great privilege for the organization and I have always made my employers recognize that no matter what they are paying me is not the true worth of my value. I let them know that I am there temporarily to fix issues and leave when God says, "Your job is done; it's time to move on." I don't have control over my time. Money does not practically motivate me, but my assignment in every organization. This is what I first discover and see to its being done.

"Look, I am coming soon; I bring my rewards with me, to repay all people according to their deeds" Revelations 22:12

I'm very conscious of the fact that I am going to give an account to God on the way I handle every office and position he has given unto me. How do we manage our flocks, marriage, children, neighbors, money, fame and other resources He has brought our way?

There are lots of synagogues all over. God knows His own. It's not by branding or size; it is not even by the philanthropic works of the assembly, neither is it by the weight of the miracles. After all, a man can give for a wrong motive, either for personal or denominational popularity. Instead, we should inquire from the mind of God, to know exactly what God wants us to do with the resources He puts in our hands. We are not meant to live our lives and running our ministries by comparing ourselves with others. We have no benchmark. The only thing that qualifies us to be true children of God is working in the Spirit. Only by this, can we please God. Any other ways of suggesting, nice ideas of men, information from the best business and leadership schools are not meant to be our guide.

"But you are not in the flesh, but in the spirit, if indeed the spirit of God dwells in you. Now if anyone does not have the spirit of Christ, he is not His." Romans 8:9

This scripture informs us that your position in any assembly is not what matters. If the spirit of God does not dwell in you, you automatically belong to the devil and the gathering of such men is a synagogue of Satan. A friend once told me that there was an assembly that people were questioning how genuine they were for God. But this local assembly was very rich, miracles happened every time, and their philanthropic work was immeasurable.

The truth of the matter is that miracles should not be the basis or parameter for knowing the true church. What about resources, knowledge and wisdom? All these were sufficient in Egypt those days. The church has been brainwashed with doctrines and messages from the pit of hell. We don't want to suffer with Christ, but we want to reign with Him. We have turned God to Father Christmas. We believe that by coming to Him all our problems would be solved.

A large percentage of the crowd that we see today, are men and women that have come to God because of the pressing issues of their lives. We have turned God into an herbalist or a magician. Our primary purpose of coming to Him shouldn't be seeing our problem solved. Whether our problems are fixed or not, He still remains the God of the universe. Our opinion does not count about His status. He doesn't need our approval to be God. He was God before the creation of the whole world, and He will still be God when the world is no more. It is great foolishness to give God conditions, as to our worship of Him. Some will tell Him, "If you don't do this particular thing for me within this period of time I will stop serving you". You have quickly forgotten that you are the clay and He is the Potter. He designs, some big, some small, and some beautiful items for men's admiration and some ugly by men's judgment. All the same, He created, everything was created to bring Him glory and pleasure.

THE ATTRIBUTES OF THE SYNAGOGUE OF SATAN

The attributes of the synagogue of Satan are enormous, yet these go beyond what can be determined by our human factors and conditions.

Secondly, the Bible says, "By their fruits you shall know them." This is also confirmed by the revelation of Jesus to John: "I know about your suffering and your poverty, but you are rich; I know the blasphemy of those opposing you. They say they are Jews, but they are not, because their synagogue belongs to Satan"(Rev.2: 9).

"Look, I will force those who belong to Satan's Synagogue those liars who say they are Jews, but are not to come and bow down at your feet. They will acknowledge that you are the one I love" Revelations 3:9

A common attribute of the synagogue of Satan is deception and falsehood that the scriptures above confirm. There are a lot of churches that have a form of Christ, but are synagogues of Satan. It is not all the time you can determine such by their name. They have a semblance of the church of Jesus, but by their principles and operations they are of the devil. They are the set of people Jesus referred to that will come on the last day, telling Him what they have done and achieved, but he would tell them, "I never knew you; depart from me, you workers of iniquity."

"But I will continue doing what I have always done. This will undercut those who are looking for an opportunity to boast that their work is just like ours. They are deceitful workers who disguise themselves as apostles of Christ. But I am not surprised! Even Satan disguises himself as an angel of light. So it is no wonder that his servants also disguise themselves as servants of righteousness. In the end they will get the punishment their wicked deeds deserve." 2 Corinthians 11: 12-15

Some of these traits of the Synagogue of Satan are:

Deception and falsehood

Deception and falsehood have eaten deep into the church, to the extent that become a norm. It is the same spirit at work in the church that makes parties not to be loyal to their marital vows. This same spirit makes leaders to suspect their followers and the followers in turn suspect their leaders on many issues.

In genuine Repentance

"For it is impossible to bring back to repentance those who were once enlightened those who have experienced the good things of heaven and shared in the Holy Spirit, who have tasted the goodness of the word of God and the power of the age to come- and who then turn away from God. It is impossible to bring such people back to repentance; by rejecting the son of God, they themselves are nailing him to the cross once again and holding him up to public shame." (Hebrew 6: 4-6). A lot of so called believers have never got to the point of repentance in their lives. Activities within these local assemblies make people feel that they are enslaved.

False Doctrine

"When I left for Macedonia, I urged you to stay there in Ephesus and stop those whose teaching is contrary to the truth. I Timothy 1:3

But some people have missed this whole point. They have turned away from these things and spent their time in meaningless discussions. They want to be known as teachers of the Law of Moses, but they don't know what they are talking about even though they speak so confidently." I Timothy 1:5-6

This is why you see some people define the Holy Spirit as an active force instead of a being, God.

Preacher of strange Gospel

"I marvel that you are turning away so soon from Him who called you in the grace of Christ, to a different gospel. Which is not another, but there are some who trouble you and want to pervert the Gospel of Christ" Galatians 1:6-7.

There are different gospels out there, just for the selfishness of the preachers. These messages are instigated by the devil and are satanic Inspired Version. Jesus preached only the Gospel of the Kingdom all through His earthly ministry. (Matthew 4:23; 9:35 and Mark 1. 14-15).

Seeker of carnal knowledge

"Because the mind is enmity against God: for it is not subject to the law of God, nor indeed can be." Romans 8:7.

When we talk about the law of God, we mean His word and will. Carnality talks about sense knowledge, information from the soulish realm. It is not possible to please God with human reasoning. It must be by the leading of the Spirit. The era of motivation has gone. Motivation, places emphasis on what a man can do, this is the season of the Spirit. Many preachers are just motivational, raising a motivational congregation, men and women that have never had any encounter with God. This is nothing but a dead church and synagogue of Satan. This has been the same strategy of the enemy. He succeeded in offering Adam and Eve's carnality for spiritual experience.

Teachers of the traditions of men

The gospel has not penetrated some places today because men have elevated their traditions, cultures and belief system over the gospel of Christ. These systems are already in operation and are even being preserved by the church and they contradict and stand against the effectiveness of the gospel of Christ in the hearts of men, community and nations.

"For there are many rebellious people who engage in useless talk and deceive others. This is especially true of those who insist on circumcision for salvation. They must be silenced, because they are turning whole families away from the truth by their false teaching. And they do it only for money." Titus 1:10-11.

"When I left for Macedonia, I urged you to stay there in Ephesus and stop those whose teaching is contrary to the truth." (1Timothy 1:3).

Devil's Advocate

This refers to the congregation of men and women who are living and working for the cause of their master, the devil, either openly or secretly. This category of people manifest their traits in different lights. The synagogue of Satan has always been a dynamic one. A layman might not be able to fully comprehend its activities. For example, Magus Anton Szandor Lavey (1930-1977) was the founder of the Church of Satan in America. This is a synagogue officially and openly established for people who want to serve and worship Satan. You can read for yourself on their website. There are many people who cannot openly declare themselves as Satanists, but all their operations are to the glory and worship of Satan. All of their activities are against the truth, that is, the word and the will of God. There are a lot of people out there who are working for the devil, but only give a nice name to their own assembly. A lot of people on a daily basis are being turned away from the truth.

"But there were also false prophets in Israel, just as there will be false teachers among you. They will cleverly teach destructive heresies and even deny the master who brought them. In this way, they will bring sudden destruction on themselves. Many will follow their evil teaching and shameful immorality. And because of these teachers, the way of truth will be slandered." 2Peter 2: 2

Some are working for the devil, but cannot openly declare themselves for the devil, so as to deceive many. Jesus warned the disciples many times to take heed to themselves, so that they would not turn away from the truth on the last day. Satan is a liar.

"These people are false apostles. They are deceitful workers who disguise themselves as apostles of Christ. But I am not surprised! Even Satan disguises himself as an angel of light. So it is no wonder that his servants also disguise themselves as servants of righteousness. In the end they will get the punishment their wicked deeds deserve." 2 Corinthians 11:13-15

It has gone so bad that someone can even use the name of Jesus and yet be a servant of the devil. In these last days, many of these shall be revealed. "He that thinks he is standing should take heed, lest he falls." The devil is aware that he has short a time, and he wants to achieve all his plans. The question is: will you stand for God till the end, even when it seems it is not convenient or will you follow the multitude to look back? It is yours to decide.

Chapter Nine

The Present-day Church

"A generation without prophetic direction will soon fall into oblivion."

Indeed the Sovereign Lord never does anything until He reveals His plans to His servants, the prophets. Everything I prophesied has come true, and now I will prophesy again. I will tell you the future before it happens.

Amos 3:7, Isaiah 42:9

The present day church is the bridge between the previous generation and the next one. Today's church cannot but get it right by living up to its responsibility and heaven's expectation. The whole world is in a mess and confusion. Professionals have failed. Men who are connected to God are the only ones with the solution in their hands. It is the visible glory upon the church that the world will see and absolutely submit to. This glory is far greater than the common miracles and prosperity.

The true breakthrough of the last days will not be of human effort or the level of intelligence, it will be by the Spirit of the Lord. The glory upon the true church is going to draw the attention of the world to the church.

We should not be carried away by this doing of God. The church is going to become a consultant, a pacesetter for the world. In large numbers, the world will come. But in the midst of this breakthrough many shall be polluted, turning the breakthrough into idols and beginning to worship them. The hearts of many shall go after the breakthrough instead of the God behind the breakthrough. When the Israelites were leaving Egypt, God created an opportunity for them to carry enough gold along. He knew that they would need it when they got to the Promised Land. He also knew that they would want to build a place of worship for him. But on their way to the Promised Land, they gave the gold to Aaron to mold an idol which they worshipped. The church must be wary of falling into the same error.

THE GREAT HAPPENINGS

In the last day church, many shall be distracted from vision to ambition. Competition shall increase, because the cares of this world will make many to miss the mark. Many shall give their worship to self. This is where motivation will come in. Many will come in; many will build their testimonies around themselves. But the Lord shall burst this balloon and their pride shall bring sorrow to them.

Also, the mighty shall fall because their confidence is in the flesh. The unknown shall become known. God is going to use the base things of the world to silence the wise, so that the universe will know that it is neither by power, nor by might says the Lord. Unusual energy shall be given to the feeble and the oppressed. The hand of God is turning the tables of the world power around. And the true church is going to showcase the glory of our King to the world.

A great darkness is coming over the earth as the prophets of old prophesied. However, in the midst of the same confusion, the church will shine and will be the light that will put illumination into the world. Many shall be killed, and God Himself shall do the killing. This death shall be in two ways. The first category is the Ananias and Sapphira (ministers who are coming into apostleship with personal agenda). Also, the Gehazi ministers will be dealt with; men who have exchanged the true prosperity for materialism. The calamity that will fall on, many will be so much that it would have been better that they did not accept the call of God.

The second category is the Moses ministers who will be taken home by God Himself. These are men who have a right heart and energy for God, but they couldn't key into the next level of the move of God. He will shut down their system by Himself, rather than have them pollute and damage His work within the Church.

Those who will decide to go all the way for Him, either for pain or pleasure, shall be preserved upon completion of the real process ordained by Him, they shall shine like stars.

There is going to be a separation between His children and His sons. The children are liabilities; committed to the laws of the Father, but they are not ready to take responsibilities and to endanger their lives for the kingdom. The sons shall be elevated. It will have nothing to do with title, position, gender, age and complexion. The words of Daniel shall come to pass: "They that know their God shall be strong and do exploits." The exploits of the last days will be for those who have the ability to hear and to do the will of the Father. The strength of great nations shall fail. David Company shall emerge; unknown men shall become known. The strength of the professionals shall fail, but the prophets shall be strong. Many businesses shall be lost; the ability of the expatriates shall expire. Innovation will be by the Holy Ghost to God's own people. This shall be the time of the fulfillment of the word: "Eyes have not seen, ears have not heard what the Lord has in store for those that love Him and also called by His name." The joy of the Lord shall be the strength of those that trust Him. There is going to be a great merger between great institutions of the world. The great strategists will fail and their strategies utterly useless, but those that are connected to the heavenly network shall be envied. It shall be a time of separation between those who serve God and those who do not. "He that has an ear should listen to what the spirit is saying to the church."

About the Book

This book reveals what heaven expects from the church. It reveals what Jesus meant by "I will build my church." It is not a critique but a standard of spiritual measurement and divine alignment as to the definition of a true church. The true church (The Ekklesia) is not a denominational gathering of any kind, whether orthodox, charismatic or Pentecostal. The true church is one, which has placed primacy on building the dispensational temple (the man) only according to God's pattern.

This book will be a great eye opener for you. You will no longer strive in the flesh any more after going through this book. The issue of competition, comparison, sense of inferiority and superiority complex, which are some of the distraction and strategies of the enemy, will be exposed. Your work and ministry with God will never remain the same. You can't read this book and still retain your old mentality and operating system. Whatever you are building for the Lord from now on shall be for the Lord's glory and according to his specifications. Personal agenda will be given up. Deeper truths and insights are made available in this book..

About the Author

Isaac K. Arikawe is the Chief Responsibility Officer (CRO) of Revelation of His Kingdom Ministries (a non-denominational teaching ministry) and the International Coordinator for Kingdom School of Ministry (a non-denominational spiritual development platform for equipping God's people for ministry work globally).

Arikawe has an apostolic ministry: he is committed to the advancement of God's kingdom on the earth and the edifying of the body of Christ to perfection. He runs the Kingdom Schools of Ministry free of charge. He also speaks regularly at conferences, leadership meetings, and churches. His books have inspired many people globally.

He is married to Temitope, an admirable medical doctor with a deep passion for God's kingdom. Arikawe currently resides with His family in Lagos, Nigeria.

Other books by the Author

THE DEAD-LIVING CHURCH

The book, "The Dead-Living Church", gives us a clear picture of what the church on earth is supposed to be as opposed to what it is today. It re-defines the concept of the church, its global positioning and its responsibilities according to the original intent of God. Jesus' declaration in Matthew 16, "I will build my church and the gates of Hell shall not prevail against it" far outweighs the theological assumptions and religious beliefs about what church is supposed to be. The truth of the matter is that the heart of Jesus is bleeding again because the church He died for and purchased with His blood has misplaced its identity and deviated from its core responsibilities. The church is now pursuing shadows, paying attention to trivialities and neglecting the things that are more important.

THE EMERGENCE OF THE SONS

A child can only be born while a son would be made. A whole lot of processes are involved - transformation, changes, growth, capacity and character development before a child can come to the point of complete resemblance of his father. The responsibility and authority lies in the hands of the sons, men and women who have grown up to a higher intimacy and integrity of heart (people of high competence in the spirit). Their major burden and focus is to see the mind of the father being established on earth. They are men and women who are taking over nations and kingdoms of our Lord (those whose hearts have been knit to the Father's). The entire hope of the father lies in the hands of the sons. They are the people that the Father can share His heart with. Sonship is not about age or title, but maturity in the spirit. Be ready to go through this process so as to be relevant in the plans and purposes of God.

BURDEN: A CATALYST FOR REFORMATION AND REVOLUTION

Every change, revolution and true reformation are a function of burden. The burden is anything that bothers you. The solution comes in the midst of great burden and concern. Nehemiah, Esther, Moses, Daniel and the Patriarchs of were able to do exploits just because they had great heaviness and burden in their hearts for discomforting situation. How many of us are ready to partner with God, making what hurts His heart to hurt our hearts? How many are ready to pray: "God, let everything that bothers you also bother me and let the burden of your heart be transferred into mine?" Until you get to this level, you would be living for yourself. The earth should not be expecting so much revolution and reformation until you and I begin to live beyond ourselves. We shouldn't be expecting a serious change except we pay the price. This book will surely open you up to a great burden in the spirit.

PROPHETIC LIVING

It is a book that talks about the needs of growing to a level of understanding the will and the mind of God per time. Deaf and dumb are not too far from deadness. Inability to hear and see from God's perspective is a function of spiritual deafness or an indication of being a bastard. It is not possible to walk in the accurate plans of God for our lives if we cannot hear from Him. God speaks per time, but until we tune our lives to this frequency, we would continue to hear wrong messages from wrong stations. This leads to the process of doing the wrong things, embracing wrong values, regardless of how nice it might look like. This book exposes you to hearing God and the benefits of hearing Him per time. Your life will never remain the same if you read it.

PROPHETIC TRANSFER OF WEALTH

There are a whole lot of resources on wealth creation, strategies, the process of making, managing and retaining it, and so on. Among all these, the world's leading business schools and colleges, professors and expatriates have written and published so much through research and forecast, yet the reality of economic crises still has a global effect on the nations without any specific solution. Many have become jobless, while many great institutions have folded up. This is not the devil at work per se, but another way of God's involvement in the affairs of men. Only those that know their God on the last day shall be strong and do exploits. There is going to be a separation between goats and sheep, between sons and slaves. Heaven is raising the end time financiers for the sake of the kingdom. There is an outpouring of grace and anointing for unusual wealth creation, transfer and management on the connected saints of the last days. This book reveals the agenda of heaven on this issue and how to be qualified to be a partaker.

THE ACCURATE IDENTITY

Many lives have been short-circuited. It is the greatest desire of the enemy to ensure that the saints live outside their true Identities. Our position in the spiritual realm is a function of the identity we carry. The impact of a man on earth is a function of his identity in the spirit. Also, the power and forces on earth and in the heavenliness are determined by the authority we have in the spirit. It is not a function of positions. Accurate identity talks about walking in the reality of redemption. Our position in Christ and our weight in the spirit are part of the things that determine our true identity. This book will provoke you to build a life in the spirit so that you can be relevant in God's move.

BUILDING FOR GLOBAL IMPACT

Man, as an offspring of God, was originally endued with the capacity and ability to operate without any limitation of any geographical location. It is an aberration to creation and the purpose for man as a spirit being to be limited by some factors. Man was originally designed with eternal software that has the ability to fix national and global issues. This means that the value of every true man should be measured by his global impact. In every man lies a hidden sound that needs to be globally echoed or heard. This book will open your eyes and propel you to building for global impact.

KINGDOMIZING THE EARTH

The earth is the only place that the awesomeness of God can be expressed. The true citizens of the kingdom live consciously everyday with this mentality. If the glory will go to God from the earth, it must be by the activities and operations of the saint through their individual callings and specialization. Up till now the earth has been forcefully hijacked, wrongly colonized, subjected and controlled by the Babylonians (wrong hands). This will continue until the sons of the Kingdom arise. This book reveals much expectations and responsibilities and consequently concerns the awakening of the kingdom citizens to their God-ordained calling. The true kingdom values must swallow up the Babylonians systems. Every opposing kingdom must be subdued and colonized for our King. This book is an eye opener and a call to contention.

OTHER BOOKS

8. The Church and the Rock (The Remnant Church

9. Prophetic Leadership

10. Apostolic Fatherhood and Mentoring

11. The Portrait of a Man of God

12. The Apostolic Rescuing of Soul

13. The Prophetic Compass of the Last Days Church

14. Understanding the Moves of God

15. Adam and Eve: Parable for Divine Union

16. The Messenger and the Message

17. Christ: The Pattern Son

18. Nehemiah: Pattern for True Apostolic and Prophetic Ministry

Kingdom School of Ministry

Introduction

The Kingdom School of Ministry is an offspring of Revelation of His Kingdom Ministry. Being a Ministry commissioned solely to the maturing (equipping) of the Body of Christ through our resources and materials—books and articles, Conferences, Seminars/Trainings, Media and Mobile Kingdom School of Ministries round the world.

The birth of the School: (KSM)

We are in a crucial season in the history of creation that times and events are testifying about. It is obvious that God is gradually bringing the age to a close. However, His intentions and purposes for creation must be fulfilled, though it tarries.

Many prophecies in regard to this have been fulfilled and some are still hanging in the air waiting for the fullness of time when the church (the Body of Christ) would rise up to her responsibilities in fulfilling the prophecies. This would be very impossible except she (body of Christ) has a prophetic understanding of the Seventh day (the completion and perfection of all things) agenda of God.

The question to be asked is, "Where is the church (the people) that will activate this prophetic agenda? Do we think this present church system, a mere religion, humanism, materialism and entertainment kind of Christianity can fit into this divine mandate?"

The Kingdom of God needs to be established, this was the center of Jesus messages on earth (scriptures), which must consequently reflect in every human endeavor.

Jesus gave the church a mandate, *"Therefore, go and make disciples of all the nations, baptizing them in the name of the Father and Son and the Holy Spirit. Teaching these new disciples (students) to obey all the commandments I have given you. And be sure of these: I am with you always, even to the end of the age."* (Matt. 28:19-20).

It is important to note that this command or mandate far outweighs our evangelical/charismatic assumption about the scriptures. It describes the entire process of turning a man into another being, **the express image of Christ** through proper training and discipleship.

The church would need more than the current knowledge to get this done. She needs the proceeding (current) truth from God to get this established. So therefore, the revelational knowledge is required.

God Himself testified to this truth, through the prophet Hosea in his book. *"My people are being destroyed because they don't know me....* Hosea 4:6 (NLT).

Meanwhile, this requires a progressive accession, continuous internal transformation, that will lead to outward transfiguration, where the scripture, Matt. 5:16 would be fulfilled. There is a need for the people of God to become apostolic/prophetic saints regardless of our individual offices in the ministry gifts. The true Kingdom must be expressed in us through a **godly lifestyle, dying to self, power and authority, right knowledge, wisdom, understanding and revelation.** So the church of Jesus Christ (locally and globally) must take pleasure in growing up into maturity, the fullness of Christ which is the Christ-like expression that is needed for his hour.

It is imperative for everyone in the fold to discover and be empowered to fulfill their heaven-given purpose for the singular aim of advancing the Kingdom of Our King on earth. This burden gave birth to KINGDOM SCHOOL OF MINISTRY (KSM).

KSM is a kingdom-based Apostolic/prophetic educational initiative that is commissioned to midwife a last-day generation of saints by teaching and training believers and to serve as a grooming center for those that are called into a specific ministerial assignment of the last days. KSM will help them to clearly discover their purpose and empower them to fulfill it. It is a place where true kingdom-class leadership are formed or developed.

KSM does not have a particular denominational affiliate, rather she is ready to partner with any ministry, a local church, groups or individuals in any form of training, seminar, or schooling for their members, workforce or family for the purpose of kingdom expression.

KSM, also is not another type of theological school or one of the traditional Bible schools, rather this school is for spiritual development and to continuously plug men and women into the very current move of God and the emphasis for now.

This school by the aid of the Holy Spirit promises life transforming modules or curriculum, that you don't find in any traditional bible school. Rather, every grandaunt will wear a new spiritual nature and mentality.

OUR MISSION

To midwife the last day remnants that have been called and chosen to finish according to God's pattern and time table.

OUR PURPOSE

To educate, train and impact believers with relevant graces to build effective lives and ministries, by leading them back to the original intention of God for creation.

OUR OBJECTIVES

- To see the saints coming into maturity and the perfecting of the Body of Christ.
- To place great emphasis on the current move of God and His kingdom reality on earth.
- To introduce and fortify the ministry gifts with apostolic and prophetic graces.
- To raise a community of believers that can resist the influx of Babylon (the system of this world) within the Body of Christ and society.

OUR FOCUS (As school, training and seminar organizers)

- The kingdom concept
- The dynamics of God's moves and His seasons on earth.
- Kingdom-class leadership development.
- Original concept of the Ekklesia (church) on earth.
- Kingdom advancement and re-definition of the church growth.
- Maturity and finishing generation.
- The minister and the ministry.

OUR FACILITATORS

KSM is not a one man show. We are blessed with men and women of God within the five-fold ministry and marketplace apostles with a special understanding and grace in the Apostolic and prophetic dimension of Christ. Teachers with practical proof of godly lifestyles and testimonies whose burden goes beyond their denominational affiliates and personal gains.

We also raise teachers from our schools and train participants

Note: KSM is a FREE of charge school and our details are on our web page. www.ksm777.org.

Contacts:
5, Bariyu Street,
Off Holy Saviour Road,
Off Osolo way,
Isolo.

+234 803 575 0747, +234 809 1705 255
+234 807 1731 856
Contact @ ksm777@gmail.com; ksm777.org
www.ksm777.org

www.ingramcontent.com/pod-product-compliance
Lightning Source LLC
Chambersburg PA
CBHW052212090526
44584CB00017BB/2182